TRANSFORMING ECONOMICS

THIRD · WAY · BOOKS

TRANSFORMING ECONOMICS

A Christian Way to Employment

Alan Storkey

First published in Great Britain 1986
SPCK
Holy Trinity Church
Marylebone Road
London NW1 4DU

Thanks are due to *New Society* and Richard Natkiel Associates
for permission to use the map 'Where the military money goes:
the north-south divide'.

British Library Cataloguing in Publication Data

Storkey, Alan
    Transforming economics. — (Third Way
    books)
    1. Unemployment — Religious aspects —
    Christianity
    I. Title   II. Series
    261.8'5   BR115.E3

ISBN 0-281-04225-X

Typeset by Pioneer, Perthshire
Printed in Great Britain by
Whitstable Litho Ltd., Whitstable, Kent

Contents

THIRD WAY BOOKS

Series Editor: Tim Dean

Third Way Books aim to explore the relation between biblical Christian faith and political, social and cultural life. SPCK and *Third Way* magazine have joined together to publish a series that will introduce some contemporary writing to a wide audience.

Third Way is an evangelical magazine which seeks to provide a biblical perspective on politics, social ethics and cultural affairs. Further details from: *Third Way*, 37 Elm Road, New Malden, Surrey KT3 3HB.

Preface

A number of different streams come together in this book and it might be helpful to describe each of them. The most immediate is a sense of shame at the indifference and complacency with which the unemployed and their dependants have been treated. When we moved from Worksop to London in 1982, we also experienced moving from daily awareness of this problem to southern cosiness and detachment. Unemployment was the greatest national problem, but the general attitude indicated that little could be done about it. There seemed to be no alternative to present policies. So this book is the result of the kind of troubled conscience which is unsatisfied with the answers it has been given. Presumably, many other people feel the same.

It reflects, too, an awareness of the extended crisis in the discipline of economics. This is partly evidenced by the fundamental levels on which economists disagree, but it is also shown in the relative impotence and otherworldliness which accompany the attempts of the discipline to be rigorous and scientific. The failure of attempts to establish an autonomous basis for economic science and to disengage positive and normative economics also reveal how deeply the subject is compromised. In this book there is not room to examine the crisis properly, because of the more immediate task, but it is important background to Part One.

Perhaps the main flow of the book is the attempt to develop further a Christian perspective on economics, taken up by various Christians in the late 1960s on the understanding that biblical revelation is a necessary prerequisite for perceiving our situation more truly. This work was opened up in Britain especially through Tony Cramp, the Shaftesbury Project, the Christian Studies Unit and more recently through various other organizations such as the Association of Christian Economists, the London Institute for Contemporary Christianity, and the Open Christian College. In 1980 I was able to spend a year as one of the Fellows at the Centre for Christian Studies at Calvin College, working on a Christian approach to economic theory. The time there with George

Monsma, John Tiemstra, Carl Sinke, Fred Graham, and with the contributions of Bob Goudzwaard, was invaluable.

It was there, as a group, that we decisively adopted an explicit institutional approach. The decision probably owed most to Dutch Kuyperian Christian thinking, and may be mildly affected by American institutional economics. Although obviously I think that a Christian normative institutional approach moves to the crux of many of the issues which the discipline needs to address, it is evident that in opening up this perspective I have had to treat lightly certain areas such as technological change. Perhaps this has led to a lack of balance in addressing the problem of unemployment. The reader will judge whether this is the case. I am also aware that judgements are made within the text about various economic positions which are not fully substantiated. These judgements are not pursued here because of the central aim of the text, but they are not made lightly and I hope that elsewhere the full grounds of the critique can be developed. Meanwhile, they remain sketchy and will leave the proponents of the positions unsatisfied. I still believe that the way we treat one another economically is the crucial matter, rather than secular trends in technology or whatever.

The book also reflects a commitment to integrated study which breaks away from the autonomy of the disciplines, and especially economics. Even to undertake interdisciplinary study is not enough, until the basis upon which the disciplines are seen to cohere is understood. Such an approach involves modifying many of the conventional definitions and boundaries, and its development has been helped by the Christian perspective on theoretical analysis developed by Dooyeweerd and others. I hope it will commend itself, especially in the face of the fragmentation of knowledge in the social sciences today.

It is also written against the background of one of the most momentous periods of change in British culture. Fundamental dogmas such as the belief that the political debate must be conducted in terms of conservatism and socialism, the faith in the infallibility of scientific knowledge, a belief in power, and faith in economic progress, are in their dotage. In many areas there are the serious problems of a degenerating society. Unemployment in this context seems to be a symptom of a deeper crisis. The political debate in the late 1980s is important, but the scale of the issues moves outside policy formulation. Where are we going? From what vantage point do we understand ourselves? The book is written with some of the excitement of a Christian who knows not only his sin and God's grace to him, but also the sheer scope of God's love for his creation, and his groaning over our waywardness. Perhaps, even, this book might be a small symptom of Christ's power to heal and restore our fractured lives. That is its biggest ambition.

While working on the manuscript I was directly in debt to Tony Cramp, Alec Storkey, Bob Goudzwaard, Andrew Brookes, Andy Hartropp, Sue Fishwick, Tim Dean, Donald Shell and Ian Hayter, who have substantially improved the book but are not bound to its views. Thank you for your considerable help. Thank you, especially, Tim Dean for your careful editorial hand, and the members of the SPCK staff for your good work. My wife Elaine is more deeply implicated, in ways which I cannot untangle and which are beyond acknowledgement.

Alan Storkey
February 1986

PART ONE
THE CURRENT ORTHODOXIES

Here we look at the most common views of unemployment. The first chapter considers why many people are so resigned to masses of people being out of work. It examines whether this approach is encouraged by some of the ways in which economic theory is seen, by our insulation from the issue and by our own interests. Rather than considering unemployment as inevitable, the chapter concludes that there may be a great deal we can do about it. However, when we turn to act, we find that the orthodox views are deeply at odds with one another. Monetarism, Keynesianism and socialism diagnose the problems differently and offer different solutions. Any study of the issue has got to wrestle with the answers provided by these three approaches and determine why they talk past one another.

The second chapter looks at monetarism. It examines monetarist policies with their recipe for fuller employment. Underlying the monetarist position is a certain view of markets which shapes the way in which the whole economic enterprise is interpreted. This view is questioned, along with the conclusions drawn from it. An alternative understanding of markets is offered which prepares the way for a new approach and allows an evaluation of monetarism and its failure to cure unemployment.

Chapter 3 focuses on Keynesianism. It stresses the differences between the approach of Keynes and the framework which was later imposed on Keynes's teaching by other economists, labelled 'Keynesian'. Some of the important characteristics of Keynes's economics are noted for later reference, but most of the chapter is an examination of the later, rather mechanical, Keynesian models and their deficiencies. Especially, the chapter notes the failure of Keynesianism to be aware of the importance of institutional breakdown in creating Britain's economic problems. Again the suggestion is that the underlying approach to economic theory leads to the wrong kind of answers.

The socialist and Marxist analysis which is then examined seems at first sight to offer a much more optimistic approach. The Labour theory of value gives work absolute priority and allows various ways in which the workforce may be misused to be identified. But this way of solving the issues actually does so by abolishing them and turns out to be unhelpful in addressing detailed problems. After looking at a Marxist view of justice, the chapter considers whether the State can be used to solve the problem of unemployment, and its failures to do so are examined.

These chapters show how confused the current debate is, but they also provide some pointers towards a more coherent approach to addressing the issue of unemployment, which is the concern of Part Two.

1: Is Unemployment Inevitable?

The Scale of the Problem

Most of us know someone who is unemployed — a friend, an ex-workmate, a relative, a neighbour, a son, a daughter or a spouse. For some of us the problem may be no closer than the memory of deciding whom we should lay off. Others may be insulated from the issue by living in a pleasant area and having a secure job. But all of us really know that the three to four million people at present unemployed are our concern. The weary succession of depressing figures, the seemingly pointless discussion of the issue, the reactions of the miners in 1984/5 to redundancies, and the decline of Britain are all concentrated into the fact that every seventh or eighth able-bodied person is out of work. We can guess what this means: the men and women who withdraw into solitude to cope with the end of their useful lives, the young people whose self-respect is strung out on a hundred or more ignored or refused job applications, the areas where so many are out of work that shops stagnate and close, or the schools where the very educational process is called in question by the single phrase, 'What's the use?' The problem is big and broods over us. What are we going to do? What can we do?

Many view large-scale unemployment at the end of the twentieth century as inevitable. The micro-chip will eliminate millions of jobs in the coming decades. Automation is reducing the workers needed for manufacturing to little more than maintenance staff. One farmworker can handle several hundred acres and service jobs are being phased out by automatic dispensers and self-service. Cheap overseas labour can easily undercut costs in many areas of traditional manufacturing. Moreover, Britain has been subject to a long-term economic decline which we have no reason to think is coming to an end. On these arguments there are bound to be millions of persons jobless at the end of the century. So goes the received wisdom.

People in earlier periods of history have been convinced of

the inevitability of unemployment, but within a few years were shaken out of their belief. When the train superseded the stagecoach, jobs disappeared on a massive scale on the turnpikes of England; when the tractor replaced the horse, the same happened on the farm. By the middle of this century the one and a quarter million jobs provided by domestic service had vanished. The way these changes have been incorporated into British economic life suggests that no technical change is an adequate ground for assuming the inevitability of unemployment. If it is assumed, it must be on some other grounds. Clearly the new technologies of micro-electronics and automation, as they are presently being developed, involve threats to many jobs. But it could be, under certain conditions, that these technologies open up work possibilities not available earlier. The argument of inevitability is self-imposed.

It is accepted in some quarters that a fall in unemployment may occur, but it is not an event which we can effectively hasten. Unemployment goes up and down, but this is largely through processes which we can do little to affect — world patterns of trade, changes in the birthrate, new explosions of consumption, and wars. There are also the fatalists and conditional optimists who say that things may get better, but it is beyond our competence to achieve full employment; we are as likely to make things worse as to improve them if we interfere. This attitude is also widespread, and it leads to people working out how to cope with unemployment rather than considering ways of eliminating it.

This book is an attack on these two positions. It holds that unemployment is not inevitable and that we can do a considerable amount to meet the problem. This is not to underestimate the seriousness of the situation. On the contrary, the oil revenue of the mid 1980s is obscuring the depths of our inability to provide work for the adult population. It does seem likely, if nothing is done, that the slowing of the flow of North Sea oil will bring worse rather than better times. In the late 1990s and beyond, Britain is likely to have a severe trade deficit which will further inhibit any possibilities of expansion and job creation. Thus the catastrophic decline in Britain's industrial base carried over from the 1970s into the 1980s will be very difficult to reverse.

Yet without in any way underestimating the challenge involved, we can consider if there are ways of addressing and even conquering the problem. If this is to happen, it will probably involve major changes of attitude, and we can begin by identifying one of the orthodoxies in current thinking which needs to be wheeled out into the public debate.

The Naturalistic Model

Many economists subscribe to a view of economics which could be called 'the tank model'. That is, the economy trundles on in whatever direction it has decided to take. The onlooker observes but can do almost nothing to alter where the great beast is going. The best that we can hope to do is observe the way in which tanks behave, take evasive action where necessary, possibly nudge it slightly in a different direction and try to make sure that it does not blow up. With good reason economics is called 'the dismal science', because much of the time it preaches that nothing can be done. Why is this? It is not that economists happen to be a bunch of neurotic, depressives. Rather, they have a predisposition which is rooted in the dominant paradigm of economic thought. In their actual process of analysis many economists assume economic affairs to be beyond human direction. This attitude is so tenacious that it is worth spending some time digging down to its roots. Where does it come from and why is it so important?

During the eighteenth century, thinkers were preoccupied with a consideration of Nature. Much of their thinking revolved around the intellectual breakthrough that came with Isaac Newton. He was interpreted in that century as having made Nature accessible to human understanding. His *Principia* had opened up the inner workings of the solar system to the gaze of all mankind.[1] Discovering the working of a mechanism became the accepted way of acquiring knowledge. This focus on understanding the natural order as a self-subsistent system was extended to the consideration of human affairs. Study was made of human nature, the nature of the State, the nature of human understanding, natural law and, of course, the nature of the economy.[2] When Adam Smith wrote *The Nature and Causes of the Wealth of Nations*, he was working largely within this framework. From this time on, the economy came to be seen as a vast, complicated natural machine which ran according to its own self-determined rules. It clanked away year after year, and the job of economists was to understand how it worked and make sure that it was regularly oiled and maintained. This, essentially, was how the classical economists approached their task throughout most of the nineteenth century.

In Europe there was an important reaction to this *laissez-faire* naturalism. European economists suggested that free trade was not naturally better than protection, that the economy should be seen in terms of its historical development and not as a mechanism, and that the State should actually guide the development of markets.[3] This emphasis was and remains different from the mainstream British and North American one, and even though we are now members of the European Community, it is still not adequately recognized.

In Britain in the 1920s and 1930s there was also a reaction created by the problems of trade and unemployment. It took two main forms. Socialists argued that the market mechanisms did not work and that their organization needed to be taken over by the State. Keynes argued that the 'natural' model of the economy could actually be seen as a special case within a broader general one. Although these theories were important, it can be argued that the naturalistic approach retained dominance in economic thinking. The late twentieth century has seen much more sophisticated approaches which have tried to avoid some of the dogmatisms built into naturalism. One, for example, was positivist economics, which claimed to be an objective, detached, scientific approach to the discipline. Yet implicitly it, too, adopted a stance similar to that of the naturalistic model. The positive economist was the onlooker, the observer, viewing without any question of engaging morally with his subject matter. His job was to examine what is the case and not what ought to be the case. The former, and only the former, was economic analysis, and when one had decided neutrally and without prejudging the issue, what the economy was like, then one could decide where it should be going and what ought to be done about unemployment. However, this neat dichotomy did not seem to work quite as planned. It was a bit like constructing a railway line and then deciding the direction in which it should point. Inevitably, it was already pointing in one direction. So when the standard neo-classical pattern of analysis assumed that the economy operated on the basis of competition and price flexibility, it also concluded that problems ought to be solved through competition and price flexibility.[4] In the end positivism, too, turned out to have its own form of naturalism. The form of observation which it assumed to be neutral and detached *was* slanted in the same way as the classical economists' position. It assumed there was a system clanking away out there waiting to be observed.

Like the naturalist position it viewed the economy from the outside, and did not allow the attitudes and values exhibited in economic activity and relationships to be questioned as part of the economic analysis. Its supposed value-free position was claimed as a virtue. In fact it turned out to be a vice. By excluding values and attitudes from the framework of economic analysis, it took for granted all the most significant economic decisions and left economists to consider the relatively insignificant technical relations in the economy. For example, there can be a technical neo-classical consideration of wage determination, but if it ignores why so many workers feel unfairly treated, why organizations fail or succeed, why work performance is often inadequate and what people view as a fair wage, the analysis is likely to be very restricted. As a result of deliberately ignoring values, their room for technical manoeuvre has become more restricted, and they are left throwing up their hands, or washing them, in an attitude of fatalistic resignation.

There is now a need, which has become urgent, to move completely outside this framework. Whatever the technical wizardry of the discipline of economics, viewing the tank from outside means that we cannot examine the way we live economically in a self-reflective and critical way. If it is *our* values, attitudes and decisions which shape the economy in which we find so much unemployment, then they need to be explicitly examined within our economic analysis. At present the prevailing attitude tends to be one of whining that the tank is out of control, when we have deliberately jumped out of the driving seat. What the economy is like is the result of *our* structuring and, if we are not too much committed to the *status quo* to consider it, restructuring of the economy is possible. In the last resort we need to be able to say that the tank should be a lorry and to have the commitment to rebuild it.

This transition is not easy. The dominant naturalistic attitude has shaped so much thinking that it is difficult to escape from it. We would do well to listen to Keynes, struggling with a form of the naturalistic model in the 1930s in order to address the problem of unemployment:

The composition of this book has been for the author a long struggle for escape, and so must the reading of it be for most readers if the author's assault upon them is to be successful,—a struggle to escape from habitual modes of thought and expression. The ideas which are here expressed so laboriously are extremely simple and should be obvious. The difficulty lies, not in the new ideas, but in escaping from the old ones, which ramify, for those brought up as most of us have been, into every corner of our minds.[5]

If we heed Keynes's words we shall recognize the problems in prising ourselves out of the thought patterns which shape our present rather fatalistic approach to unemployment. It involves living dangerously with new ways of thinking, crossing boundaries which many assume to be unbridgeable, and even questioning whether the way we live is right. But if we are serious about unemployment, that is the least we can do.

Motives in Economic Theory
Nothing is quite what it seems. Economic theory, it might appear, is the triumph of better thinking over poorer. It should on this view be subject to continual amelioration. Is this what is happening? It may not be. We may at any period merely be getting the theory that we want, the theory which suits us. Of course, there is an academic debate, arguments flow, and certain positions gain ascendancy, but *why* they become dominant is still an open question. Without in any way dismissing any of the detailed arguments, it behoves us to consider what we *want* to believe in economic theory. It is possible that this exercise will give us clues as to whether a process of wish fulfilment is going on. Put baldly, if the theorists conclude that it is not possible to do anything about unemployment, it may be because it is in their interests to do

nothing. To appreciate this point we need to look at one of the great social changes of the fifty years since the 1930s.

During the 1930s there was a massive working-class majority. Many still voted Conservative or even Liberal, but there was no doubt that the political weight lay with this group. Moreover, it experienced deep solidarity with the unemployed; they, too, were not far from the lot of the Jarrow marchers. The unity was reinforced by the moral imperatives which had grown within the Labour and Union movements. Tackling unemployment, even though there was a slow response in the 1920s and 1930s, was a majority democratic movement. It was clear that Beveridge, Attlee, Gaitskell, Butler and Macmillan reflected a popular desire for a full employment economy. There was a decisive commitment that servicemen and women should return after the Second World War to jobs and not enforced idleness.

Now the position is different. The majority, by a large margin, is middle class. Income level, job security, house ownership, pensions, job expertise, salary increments and so on indicate that they are unlikely to experience solidarity with those who have little to sell but their labour and cannot even sell that. The life situation of two-thirds of the population is within the secure and well-paying world where major economic difficulties are taken care of. This is reflected in some unions. Often the members are in skilled responsible jobs which command high levels of pay. These unions are more like professional associations and are not likely to reflect solidarity with unskilled and unemployed members of the labour market.

Unemployment is therefore a distanced reality. Although there is a public rhetoric of concern, in the actual areas of debate and policy formation there is little direct knowledge or involvement. The Labour Party is caught between its commitment to the new affluent unions and the unemployed. The Conservatives hope the problem will stay north of Watford. The SDP and Liberals have made some public response to the issue, but with little clout. Economists as a profession are more involved with the academic and business communities than with the workless. Most of us are better off with lower rates of inflation and higher pay differentials. Clearly, on the grounds of self-interest, a lot of us could happily ignore the issue. It is comfortable to accept the arguments which justify doing nothing and to believe that we understand why unemployment is inevitable. In fact we may have constructed an elaborate code of self-justification, a bypass round the city of unemployment along which we can happily drive each morning to work. We can be secure in the knowledge that the unemployed will have little political power and scarcely an effective voice for the rest of the century. They have become marginal. The rhetoric of concern might cloak a distaste for actually facing the problem.

If this is the situation for most of us, we should recognize the inbuilt bias to complacency. We might consider changes as long as they do not make too many demands on us. The policy which is likely to be acceptable in this situation might be one which purports to give a long-term solution to the problem, but which in the meantime does not really affect the position of the comfortable majority. If we buy our policies like this, our concern with unemployment might be more apparent than real. We do not tackle the issue, because we do not want to.

The Definition and Scope of Economics

There is another question lurking beneath the surface of this discussion. The naturalistic model provided the initial framework for twentieth-century economic science, but during this century most economists have believed their analysis to be sufficiently scientific to end the debate over the definition of economics. It was merely an issue which belonged to the infant development of the discipline. We note, however, that economists differed markedly in what made their work scientific.[6] Some claimed to be dealing only with facts and what could be inferred from the data, others based it on the irrefutability of their mathematics, and others on the technical relationships to which they confined themselves. One of the interesting developments of the last twenty years is the way these claims to be scientific have disintegrated.[7] It is an interesting story, but one which we cannot examine fully here. Our concern is with the way in which these supposed technical, value-free ways of obtaining knowledge have given economists terms of reference which have seriously constrained the discipline. The attempts to be scientific have actually proved a hindrance.

Consider one of the most famous and important definitions of scientific economics. Robbins saw the discipline as being 'the science which studies human behaviour as a relationship between ends and scarce means which have alternative uses'.[8] Robbins saw the subject as capable of technical, value-free development as a behavioural science. Ends themselves could be pushed outside the boundary of the discipline, which could concentrate on the conditions under which ends would be met.[9] Extra-economic ends are met by various patterns of consumption which are made possible by the scarce means available. Labour is obviously a part of the production process, the means by which these ends are met. However, once it is granted that work, an economic activity, is for many people an *end* which they greatly desire, this whole conception of economics breaks down. Unemployment is now no longer a technical problem, and the end of providing jobs becomes an inescapable part of economic analysis. This view of value-free economics founders and the neat boundary to economic science falls flat.

The same kind of issue crops up in many different forms. Theoretical differences on unemployment turn out to be substantial differences of perspective and value built into the theory. Implicitly the questions are raised: What, if anything, makes economics a science? how is the discipline separated from the rest of life? can values be excluded from the discipline? can the framework in which the theory is formulated properly address the problem of unemployment? Everyone who is awake in economics today must address these issues, for unemployment challenges the very identity of the discipline.

The Main Positions on Unemployment
In the next chapters we shall be considering the three main policy positions which dominate current responses to unemployment. They constitute the elements in the debate to which most people automatically refer, and it is important to be aware of these different positions for a number of reasons. One issue is why they seem to talk past one another without

11

common ground and a common frame of reference. Another is whether the naturalistic paradigm has influenced them in decisive ways which lead to a kind of fatalism. The third, and obviously the most important, is whether any of these policy positions can lead to a substantial and sustained fall in unemployment.

The first position is monetarism. It has a long history with a focus on the way in which the money supply is related to the level of prices. If the economy is suffering inflation, and if the main cause of unemployment is inflation, then the way to prevent unemployment is to control the money supply firmly, so that the economy can settle down into a balanced state, where all those who want jobs at the going wage can get them. This approach was quite strong in the 1920s when it fuelled the return to the Gold Standard under the Chancellorship of Churchill in a period when the value of money (and of loans) increased quite substantially.[10] It regained support with the Conservative governments of the 1980s after a long period of eclipse.

Monetarists differ on how inflation is translated into unemployment. The most usual argument stresses the overpricing of labour. When wages are higher than they should be, employers are not willing to employ as many people as want jobs and there is unemployment. The same result may occur through international competition; if wages push up the costs of British exports, then jobs will be lost in export industries or in those hit by cheaper imported goods. Why have wages been too high? Some monetarists highlight the way in which government expenditure has been excessive and has had to be financed by borrowing and printing money. Consequently, the value of money has fallen and given people all kinds of false expectations about wages and income. These expectations have led to inordinate wage demands, and until the economy settles down to realistic wage levels, there will be many who are priced out of the labour market, though not necessarily through their own fault. Another focus is the monopoly power of the unions, who have been able to enforce very high settlements through threat. Until these unrealistic elements have been purged out of the economy and it is able to settle down to an ordered pattern, the problem will continue. Other monetarists emphasize the

12

growth in the public sector which results when governments print and borrow money. The outcome, they argue, is that manufacturing and investment get squeezed, and the private sector becomes depressed.

The second position, Keynesianism, was based on the recognition that the government, by spending money, could generate income and employment for those out of work. At its simplest, if the government built new roads, this would both provide extra jobs and the resultant income would in turn generate more jobs. By careful management of its income and expenditure the government could control what the level of employment should be and make sure it was close to full employment. The key to full employment was therefore an equilibrium in the level of income in the economy, which would guarantee a level of activity at which nearly everyone was fully employed. There was therefore a contrast, and substantial inconsistency, between the monetarists' emphasis on prices and the Keynesians' emphasis on national income levels.

During the 1950s and 1960s Keynesianism seemed to work quite well. Government spending was a source of growth and produced, it appeared, high levels of employment and consumption. For a while the depression of the 1930s was left firmly behind in twenty years of prosperity. However, this policy then seemed to be linked with worsening crises in foreign trade, inflation and fiscal policy, and generating employment through increased government expenditure seemed to be less effective. Eventually criticism of this approach hardened into the policy of monetarism.

Third, socialism had taken its main direction from Marx in mounting a critique of capitalism. The latter, it is argued, is a system which contains the seeds of its own destruction, and it is one which automatically tends to create and maintain unemployment, both because of its own dynamics and also as part of a strategy for keeping the power of employees firmly constrained. The tendency of international capitalism to use cheap Third World labour also undermines domestic employment. Somewhere along the line this position emphasizes the way in which capital appropriates earnings which should accrue to the workers. This both undermines the workers' position and independence and also leads to patterns of underconsumption in the economy. Among Marxist and socialist economists there are a variety of ways in which these arguments are formulated, but the outcome is usually a demand for a different focus to the attack on unemployment.

Socialists, recognizing that private employers are under no obligation to provide employment and often do not seem very keen to do so, have focused on the key role of the State. The unemployment of the 1930s following the Wall Street Crash showed the inability of capitalism to provide the jobs that people need. Consequently, the State had to take up the responsibility of employment, directly if necessary. This might mean taking over industries, so that they can be made to pursue socially responsible employment policies and it might mean funding more jobs out of taxation, but the State's controlling responsibility has to give an answer to a problem which will not be met by the private sector. This argument seemed dated in the prosperous years of the 1950s and 1960s, but it is at the present time coming back into contention again.

The way in which these positions speak past one another is probably evident to most of us, but why they do is not so clear. At one level various interest groups pick up a policy which suits them and fail to hear counter-arguments. The City has traditionally wanted the constraints of its money markets to dominate public policy, and listens only to monetarism. The unions want expansion of employment and the clout it gives to employees, usually through Keynesian means, and do not hear arguments about restraint on public expenditure. Socialists emphasize State activity and ignore ways in which other kinds of employment might be hindered. At another level there has been partisanship among economists: there are those who refuse to consider counter-arguments and who accept only the special pleading of their own group. Monetarists refuse to consider whether the fall in inflation might have more to do with the damping of expenditure than with the price of money. Keynesians refuse to consider whether the decline of private investment follows from public-sector borrowing. Socialists do not consider the lack of public sector accountability. Academically, though perhaps not in public political debate, there is some hope that this kind of partisanship can be overcome. But beneath this level there

14

are other and deeper conceptions from which the proponents talk past one another.

At the risk of simplifying a little, we could say that monetarists consider markets to be good; socialists see them as bad. Keynesians view government intervention as good; monetarists do not. The latter see money as important, while Keynesians and socialists consider it insignificant beside the 'real' economy. Monetarists view the future with optimism; the others do not. Keynesians see the mixed economy as viable; socialists do not. They in turn identify widespread exploitation; monetarists do not, unless they see the State as exploitative. These differences are deep, even when cast in detailed technical arguments.

In the following three chapters we shall be considering these positions. Already, we can see problems ahead, for they each demand to be considered in their own terms, which are, on the whole, mutually incompatible. Clearly, we want to see how they address the issue of unemployment, but at the same time we can claim the freedom to interpret these approaches in other terms than they assert for themselves. For, to use Kuhn's terms of reference, there is now an awareness that the differences between these positions are evidence of paradigms which are at odds with one another. Something akin to a paradigm shift, a basic realignment in the way economics is seen, is under way.[11] The discipline no longer has a coherent framework for handling issues like unemployment. If this is the case, we need the freedom at least to consider an alternative paradigm.

Notes

1. The emphasis here is on the Enlightenment's interpretation of Newton, not his own position. See P. Gay, *The Enlightenment: An Interpretation,* vol. 2 (Wildwood House 1973), pp. 126–66.
2. The case is made in P. Hazard, *European Thought in the Eighteenth Century* (Penguin 1965).
3. For example, in the work of List, the historicist school of Schmoller and others and Bismarckian nationalist economics. After the Methodenstreit there was still a strong resistance to most forms of British naturalism. The rationalist traditions were more Kantian and subjective.
4. This raises the obvious problem of why the prescription should

be needed if the observational base is correct. The deeper fallacy is the impossibility of the positive/normative divide in knowledge of the human sciences.

5. J. M. Keynes, *The General Theory of Employment, Interest and Money* (Macmillan 1936), p. viii.
6. See B. Caldwell, *Beyond Positivism* (Allen and Unwin 1982) and M. Blaug, *The Methodology of Economics* (Cambridge University Press 1980) for two assessments of the philosophy of economic science.
7. F. Suppe, *The Structure of Scientific Theories* (University of Illinois Press 1977) for a good description of the collapse of the 'Received View'. My work on 'Epistemological Foundationalism in Consumption Theory' will be a study of this theme.
8. L. Robbins, *The Nature and Significance of Economic Science*, 3rd ed. (Macmillan 1984), p. 16.
9. ibid., pp. 24–32.
10. The effects of this deflation on the transfer of wealth and income were somewhat similar to those described in later chapters.
11. T. Kuhn, *The Structure of Scientific Revolutions* (University of Chicago Press, 1970). Throughout, the word 'paradigm' is used in a straightforward sense as providing a framework for understanding economic life. The epistemological and methodological issues raised by Lakatos and others will largely be ignored.

2: Monetarism and the Naturalistic Model

The Monetarist Diagnosis

During the 1980s we have all become aware of the strong influence exerted over public policy in Britain by the monetarism of the Conservative Government. It has determined what should or should not be done, in a powerful and consistent way. The broad direction of the policy can be summarized in the following terms. Monetarism focuses on the relationship between the amount of money in the economy and the level of inflation. Other things being equal, more money means higher prices as the value of money goes down. The process can be described in the following terms. If the government spends more than it raises in taxes, it can meet the difference by printing more money. The effect of this is multiple: it increases the government's control over private resources, devalues private savings, makes borrowing in the wider economy temporarily easier and advantageous, potentially devalues the currency, and leads to inflation through an expansion of bank credit. However, it can also meet the deficit by borrowing more. This has other effects. It leads to 'crowding out', the process whereby so much money is used in lending to the government that there is little left for private investment, and it also leads to higher interest rates, and a higher national debt. As the cost of paying interest on the debt rises (both through a larger debt and higher interest rates), so governments are tempted to inflate to bring down the real value of the debt. Whatever the combination of printing money and borrowing, it brings distortions in the value of money and prices which inevitably have to be met in higher interest rates, the decline in private investment and the loss of jobs. In the 1980s we have inherited the results of the lack of control over expenditure shown in the 1970s, and we must therefore correct this underlying weakness and restore the economy to health.

To combat this situation the government should exercise strict control over government spending, so that the Public

Sector Borrowing Requirement can be brought down. If it firmly controls the amount of money and government debt in the economy, it will be able to eliminate inflation and high interest rates. This will allow business to assess accurately its costs and prospects. Because there is no additional burden of heavy public-sector expenditure, firms will be in a position to expand. Wages will return to realistic levels, and unions which have in the past been in the business of price 'fixing' by bargaining for the wages of their members, will now find that wages are fixed in open-market terms, making a lot of their activities redundant. On the basis of realistic wage levels, employment will be able to pick up.

This central aim is backed up by other emphases. A denationalization programme has been set in motion, because, it is argued, the public sector does not operate in the stiff breezes of market competition and has therefore tended to be inefficient. Moreover, a decrease in public expenditure allows a programme of business and personal tax cuts, which will provide incentives for an expansion in the private sector. Further, the money markets, which have previously been heavily policed by governments will, if the money supply is properly controlled, be free to operate unfettered, with interest rates finding their own level and a more efficient capital market. This set of policies has dominated thinking and practice in Britain for most of the 1980s. A similar view has also been influential in Europe, and so we would do well to recognize the weight of this approach in the world economy. How are we to understand it?[1]

Clearly, this set of policies is appealing to an underlying model. This is why it does not offer a direct solution to the problem of unemployment. The instant cure, it says, is wrong. What is needed is a return to an underlying healthy state in the economy. It is therefore this state of natural health which we must consider. We note, not in a dismissive way but in order to give fair treatment to other positions, that this healthy state is not something which we now see. It is an idea, a powerful mental construction by which many are guided. This model is of the naturalistic market. Markets, it is believed, naturally work best. They are efficient, flexible, fair, encourage personal freedom and initiative and respond most effectively to changes in economic life.[2] There is evidence

18

for this position in the relative inflexibility of East European controlled economies, and even in the wide distribution of resources which has occurred in the free-market West. It cannot be quickly dismissed, and if markets work, then unemployment is best solved through the operation of stable markets and, especially, a free labour market.

The Labour Market

Let us look more closely at the model of the labour market which is envisaged within this naturalist perspective. There is, it is argued, a market for labour which determines the levels of employment and wages. If it operates naturally, without interruption or distortion, there will be an equilibrium at which those who want to work at the going rate will get work. The going rate is largely determined by the productivity of the workers, and as long as workers are prepared to work at a rate of pay which roughly corresponds to their productivity, they will find employment, provided the market is not distorted. Yet, it is argued, our recent history has seen considerable distortions. First, unions have used collective power to bargain for rates above the level of productivity. Second, overstimulated demand and inflation have encouraged borrowing and giving in to wage demands. There are many more sophisticated formulations of the problem, but the 'Marshallian' model effectively tells the tale and illustrates the basic assumptions. The model sees a market in terms of two groups, consumers and producers who create patterns of demand and supply in relation to price. Generally, the higher the price, the smaller the quantity which consumers wish to purchase and the more suppliers will bring to the market. Somewhere there is an equilibrium price at which the market is cleared. Here is the naturalistic view of the market for labour. See Figure 1.

Monetarists believe that wages have been pushed too high and they are waiting for the natural equilibrium and full employment to be restored.

So the market rules. Or does it? Obviously, the model outlined above is simplistic. The productivity of workers is difficult to establish individually, since their work reflects patterns of co-operation. Further, the cost involved in going to where the work might be is often considerable, and may

19

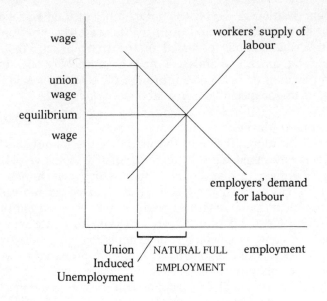

wage

workers' supply of labour

union wage

equilibrium wage

employers' demand for labour

Union Induced Unemployment

NATURAL FULL EMPLOYMENT

employment

Figure 1

prevent people taking up work. More generally, the smoothly climbing supply curve obscures the fact that some people need a job at any reasonable wage rather than just being prepared to supply more labour at a higher wage. The simplicity of the diagram could be hiding a lot of personal anguish. But allowing for a whole range of qualifications, is this roughly what is going on? Does this diagram help explain the cause of unemployment? The last thing we want to do is quibble about something so important. But there is also another question. Does accepting that unemployment has been induced by excessively high wage levels entail accepting the whole monetarist package? All of these issues really hang on the question of how markets are understood.

The Naturalistic View of Markets
Naturalist and monetarist economists believe in the automaticity of markets. We hear of 'market forces', or, in more sophisticated language, of 'determinate solutions'. The Market, spelt with a capital M, is the mechanism, which if

20

allowed to operate freely, sorts out problems like unemployment. In the previous chapter the naturalist model was described as the 'tank' view of the economy. It trundled on, and the important thing to do was respect the way it worked and not get run over. To tackle it head on would be the height of folly. Yet what is this determinate system of market forces? In what sense are *they* the arbiters of economic activity? In what sense are prices, or the level of output, or the level of employment determined by the market? On reflection, the supposed automatic operation of markets is not quite what it seems. If the Conservatives have had to work hard to restore these markets, there is already an element of discretion in them. We can go further and say that if *our* economic activity and decisions, including those of the politicians, shape markets, then all of this determinist language is a mirage, a reification of what we control. This does not solve our problems, but it does help us to see things in a new light. The 'tank' has run over us and we are still standing up!

Once we break away from this naturalist conception, it is possible to see markets in a new light. They are actually normative constructions, based on beliefs about how trading should take place, which *we* are responsible for, rather than autonomous forces. Monetarists believe that if markets are to operate fairly and without distortion, the value of money must be stable and predictable. If, however, they are going to discuss their normative commitment properly, they must be prepared to consider comprehensively what market structures *should* be like, rather than bowing down before the automaticity of markets. In defining the parameters necessary to achieve price stability monetarists are formulating an important policy goal, but it is one that takes its place alongside other normative considerations. It may, or may not, be more important than the others, but that is a question of deciding our priorities in living, not of accepting a take-it-or-leave-it package deal. If monetarists are committed to seeing stable markets as 'good', they must allow the possibility of a wider normative evaluation of markets. They have left neutrality and value-freedom far behind.

Second, we can also move away from the idea of *the* market. If markets are constructed according to a complex mixture of priorities and norms, then, rather than one market, what we actually have is the possibility of many kinds of markets with different emphases and ways of operating. Sadly, one has to conclude that economists have largely ignored this important reality merely because they want models which can easily be handled mathematically. Markets can have long or short time horizons, depend on customer loyalty or fickle consumers, and can have competition on the quality of goods or prices or can eliminate competitors. They can be consumer orientated or producer orientated, and there have been complaints throughout the 1980s that the structure of the agricultural markets in the European Community has been too producer orientated. Markets can also be pro-capitalist, in the sense that they allow full expression to dominant companies, or pro-free enterprise in that they allow the fullest opportunity for free access and competition in the market. Contrary to what is widely assumed by the Conservatives, capitalism and free enterprise are probably divergent aims. When we recognize this reality, we are able to ask the deeper question, namely, what particular kinds of market have been encouraged within the monetarist conception of things?

It also allows us to question another fundamental dogma associated with the naturalistic model of the market. This holds that the supply and demand sides of the market are independent; even if one buyer or seller dominates the whole of its side of the market, the assumption remains that they operate independently, and the market outcome is determined by an impersonal resolution of the forces. This aspect of the naturalistic model is sheer fantasy. It embodies a belief that nobody responds to the market as an organic whole. This assumption may have been valid when markets were dispersed and casual. Now, however, they are highly organized. They often have important regulative institutions; many people are employed to analyse and assess the market as a whole; politicians, as we have seen, have strong policy views on the operation of the whole market; and many organizations have developed strong market strategies. How is this possible, if markets are determinate, impersonal structures? Clearly, it is not, and the myth should be dropped. The activities of farmers in relation to the European Community's agricultural policy should have made this point long ago. We can then recognize that many economic agencies actually decide what markets should be like and put their beliefs and policies into practice. Moreover their view of the structure of markets must necessarily be normative, an overall conception of what markets should be. Again the natural, value-free approach founders.[3]

Another important dogma associated with the naturalistic market model is the supremacy it gives to *price*. This is so fundamental that we must spend some time examining the nature of this assumption. First let us look at the idea of the price mechanism as that which gives stability in the economy as a whole. Price creates, it is argued, overall equilibrium, including employment equilibrium. Keynes attacked this position in the 1930s by switching the focus to income, and once we remove price from its natural neo-classical pedestal, it is possible to see that there are many other possible forms of equilibrium and disequilibrium. Price, income, wealth, stocks, institutions, money and employment are all subject to disequilibrium and equilibrium, and it is a groundless assumption that stability in one system will lead to stability in others. Indeed we cannot even assume that instability in one system will lead to disequilibrium in another; if movement along a unit-elasticity demand curve can lead to a change in price but not in income, then in principle anything is possible. So a movement towards 'price' equilibrium may be quite permanently accompanied by disequilibrium in income, wealth, stocks, institutional life and, of course, in employment. Unless we take into account all the dynamic movements in the economy, including those generated by institutions, population and attitudes, we are likely to find that the hoped-for price equilibrium is an illusion. Indeed, the failure of the Conservatives to confine money supply growth to single figures during 1984/5 highlights the problem. The priority given to price equilibrium leads to a presumption that much more complex economic behaviour is 'basically' responding to price. This is such a fundamental misunderstanding that by itself it explains the failure of the monetarists to get to grips with unemployment. The unemployed worker, the bankrupt firm, the highly successful new industry, and the government are all only partly responding to price in major decisions which they take. Why pretend otherwise?

The same problem occurs at a microeconomic level. Why do people buy a particular good? Often *the* reason will be because they like it, or to save time, or because they need it in a certain situation. The 'determining' factor in their decision will not be price, which they might not even notice, but these other concerns which they have. Naturalistic economics insists, however, on seeing price as determinate, even if the qualification is made that other things be held constant. This is an elementary fallacy. Because goods are or are not sold at a certain price, it does not mean that they are or are not sold *because* of their price. The reality, as we shall see in detail later, is that most people are prepared to buy and sell over a considerable range of prices. This fact is of such importance that the tenacity of the neo-classical fixation on determinate prices needs explaining.

One simple explanation is that the emphasis continues partly because naturalist economists need solutions. Without linear price functions they would be forced into forms of analysis, like normative analysis, which their favourite tools would be incapable of handling. For we have to face the inadequacy of many logical and mathematical frameworks in handling time and dynamic analysis. The resultant exchange price becomes the antecedent explanation of the exchange, creating all kinds of circular arguments. Sometimes these weaknesses are sidestepped with an assumption that other things are equal. The actual effect is to lift the analysis increasngly into an unreal world, for other things never are equal. To assume a determinate outcome on the basis of ignoring major aspects of our economic life can only lead to entirely unrealistic results. Many conclusions obtained within this framework are entirely spurious in the determinate role they give to price. This does not mean that price is not important, but we need a way of considering *how* important it is, and what its fuller market context is, and what we might do to change the situation.[4]

Once we challenge the underlying paradigm with its dogmas, the specific commitments of monetarism can be placed much more easily in context. Markets are not merely impersonal forces. There is no such thing as *the* market, but many different markets, and far more is involved in them than price solutions. These facts crucially influence the way in which the labour market and unemployment are seen, as well as the monetarist policies. In order to consider these more carefully, we need an alternative market model which allows us to consider whether price is a tight constraint, how groups pursue market strategies, which normative views shape the way in which markets develop and whether market policies at present help or hinder employment.

A Discretionary Market Model

The naturalistic approach to markets ignores the values which shape markets, the strategies pursued in them, the norms through which they function and the constraints on participation. What we need therefore is a model of markets which explicitly recognizes that price and other factors do not determine markets, but are constraints within them. Then we are in a position to consider what policies, areas of discretion and values actually operate within these markets. Fortunately, this can be done with an adaptation of the Marshallian model.

Let us begin with a simple but very important point. We have already noted that consumers often decide to purchase specific items, and then see what is the lowest price available. The range of prices over which they would be prepared to purchase is often quite considerable. For insignificant items in the budget it may be 100 per cent or more, but usually it could be in the range of 5 per cent to 50 per cent. What is traditionally called a demand curve is actually a demand band, bounded by price constraints within which there is considerable discretion. We also note that the neo-classical concern with summing the purchases of one good across the buying population to construct measures of commodity-related elasticity has meant that the variations in price sensitivity of different consumer groups has often been ignored. Thus, one could construct a 'thrift' index, which might show that dual-career couples who do not have the time to shop around are much less price sensitive than single breadwinner families, or that people seem to be more careful when spending their own money than that of someone else. In this way, not only is the traditional demand curve a band rather than a line, but the width of the band is an important economic variable.[5]

What we have concluded about the price demand function

25

similarly applies to the other side of the market. Producers market goods and services with constraints on the prices they can charge, but with considerable flexibility within those constraints. They normally respond to factors like the policy of competitors, the financial position of customers, changes in government policy and the value customers place on their product. If producers are committed to a certain level of output they must show this flexibility with respect to price. So we must explicitly recognize that many producers have considerable discretion over the prices they could charge for their goods, and many non-price considerations, like keeping the workforce fully employed, could and do affect the policy they adopt.[6] Thus we conclude that in both demand and supply functions there is a (variable) discretionary space within which important strategic decisions are made. This fundamental point can be made by the following elaboration of the Marshallian framework of market analysis.

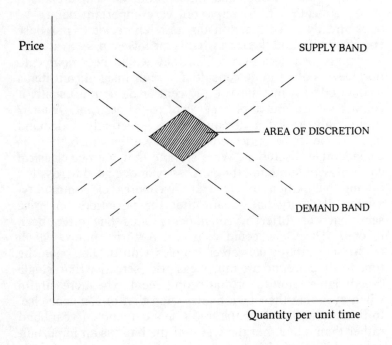

Figure 2

26

This move allows us to break from all the assumptions about the determinate effects of price, including, of course, the rate of interest, which have dogged neo-classical and monetarist analysis, and to consider explicitly the strategies adopted in the area of discretion. As a result we can actually discuss the full human policies adopted in markets, and whether they represent the right priorities or not. We can discuss the norms which operate within markets, the responsibilities which are exercised and the overall structuring of these important institutions.

At the same time this position allows us to respond to a point often made by Conservatives and downplayed by radical economists. There are price constraints, and often they are tight; undoubtedly, firms have often priced themselves out of export markets by ignoring them. By explicitly considering how wide the bands are, that is, the price discretion which companies, consumers and governments have, we are able to examine where price constraints are most important. This is a major breakthrough in what is at present an ideological deadlock where the importance of price is either denied or asserted, but not assessed. It may be that because of poor export performance and weak domestic demand companies may have a very limited area of discretion now which could open up later. Rather than dismissing price theory, there is a framework in which it can be viewed more strategically.

Market Strategies
What, then, are the possible strategies which can be adopted towards markets, given that this area of discretion exists? One extremely important one is *demand withdrawal*. This is an antagonistic rather than a co-operative policy. If consumers withdraw demand, they are able to reduce the income of suppliers, and when suppliers are not well organized, prices and sales will tend to fall. When prices have fallen, if suppliers give priority to raising their income, and if consumers follow a policy of high price sensitivity, the suppliers can be persuaded to provide more at a lower price. In this case the demand strategy is the dominant one; it shapes the conception of the way the market should work.

27

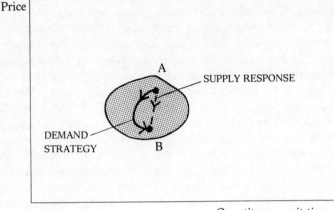

Figure 3

This strategy could be very important in relation to the labour market. If firms and governments exercise their discretion in this way in the demand for labour, it is possible for unemployment to be used as a policy to achieve reductions in real wages. The strategy is more likely to work if the area of discretion in the demand for labour is greater than the one on the supply side. This in turn is especially likely if workers are heavily dependent on a certain level of income. While monetarist orthodoxy declares such a policy to be impossible, we discover that using unemployment to force down wages is feasible and probably has been done. It may be that wages should be lower in several areas, but to hide behind the naturalistic market when pursuing that policy is not entirely honest.

The strategy could also affect many Third World producers, who can be forced onto this income constraint very easily. Since the level of effective demand in the West can be controlled through governments and the multinationals who are the 'consumers' of Third World primary products, it is quite conceivable that the prices of these products have been pushed down to the bottom of the area of discretion.

There are a number of other antagonistic market strategies.

28

One is *supply stimulation*. Consumers increase demand to raise prices, so that investment will take place which will then lead to a long-term glut in the market with low rates of return and low prices. Another is *stockpiling*. If consumers are able over a period of time to stockpile a commodity, then they achieve a degree of market independence, in that they are able at any one time both to supply and consume the commodity. The West has pursued this policy since 1973 in stockpiling oil. The threat of expanded supply can continually act as a component in the market situation. We note that the meaning of the stockpile, whether it is a threat, a reserve, a way of maintaining demand during slack periods or whatever, fits with different market strategies. Another well-tried strategy is *price reduction* to aid market penetration. A low price induces consumer conversion to a pattern which then becomes a lifelong commitment. It may be using a certain cosmetic or a large-frame computer system. All of these policies are a recognizable part of business life, but are excluded from conventional economics.

Specifically, we need to ask whether this gives an alternative view of inflation to that which is suggested by the monetarist analysis. It is possible that all kinds of groups have been using their scope in different markets to push up prices as new discretionary power to do so has become available to them. How could that new power become available? There are many ways: new monopolistic positions, growing control of markets, scarce skills, internal control of organizations, power over public-sector operations, consumer dependence, technological dependence, the reduction of consumer choice and a deliberate choice of inefficiency and higher prices. It could be that inflation, rather than having its roots in the quantity of money, is located in the self-serving abilities of various organizations and the scope they have to exercise these tendencies. There may have been a systematic overall movement to the top left-hand part of the area of discretion which becomes, in the longer term, a self-fulfilling trend.[7]

However, we should not just dwell on antagonistic strategies, for also common in markets, indeed basic to them, are co-operative ones. Producers and consumers work together so that the optimum result may come out of the transaction.

A communal strategy of lower pricing is mutually reinforcing as wages and other costs stay down. There is something of a cosmic joke in this process of co-operation. Monetarists and Conservatives are committed on the basis of their naturalist economic philosophy to argue that restraint and co-operation are in one's self-interest. But this is patently not the case. Self-interest is better served by exploiting the situation in the ways outlined above. Yet the outcome of this attitude, at the heart of Conservative philosophy, is nonco-operation, a breakdown of service and care, decline and a decomposition of the division of labour. There is no way in which the self-interested philosophy can be rationalized into a successful strategy. In the end it must just produce its bitter fruit. *The* way is to love one's neighbour as oneself, whether in the provision of a car park for the customer, in thoughtful packaging or in opening up new low-cost products for the consumer. These possibilities for co-operation, help and service are present, and we should not ignore the formative influence that they have on the development of the economy and on employment.[8]

The conclusion which can be drawn from this framework of analysis is that unemployment is not to be understood as the necessary determinate outcome of market 'forces'. Rather, it has grown up within the context of a variety of market strategies, many of which have been destructive and job-degenerate. The response which this situation requires is a consideration of how markets can be structured to encourage and provide employment and what use should be made of the discretion which there is in labour and other markets to meet this aim.

An Evaluation of Monetarism
This perspective helps us to see monetarism in a new light. The market in funds available for borrowing and lending is not as tightly defined by the money supply as the monetarists suggest. The discretion exercised by bankers in the availability of funds, in the speed of circulating money, in patterns of borrowing, and in the particular market for funds which institutions choose, all show, as most economists recognize, that the money supply control does not determine the market. Nor is the 'price' of money, the rate of interest, definitive in

30

patterns of borrowing and lending. Overseas holders of sterling will take note of other factors like the prospects of the British economy, the effectiveness of the government, likely exchange rate trends and the safety of British or overseas holdings. Possibly, for example, the movement over to floating exchange rates has increased the pattern of discretionary holding of funds and has made the conventional monetary analysis far less applicable than it would have been two decades back. This should lead us to move away from the idea that a tight control on the money supply will automatically cure inflation to an examination of the strategies and priorities of institutions in the City and the wider economy. If these shape responses in the market, although there may be temporary falls in the level of inflation in periods of depression and tight money, when the right kinds of conditions exist again, the old pressures will reassert themselves. We cannot retain any longer a belief that the whole price system can be steered by the money supply.

We can also recognize another problem. The inability of the Conservative Government to reduce the Public Sector Borrowing Requirement and hold down the money supply in the mid 1980s, although this was their declared policy, and despite massive sales of public assets, shows the necessary dependence of monetary policy on other areas. As unemployment has increased, the tax yield has fallen and payments on unemployment and other benefits have increased. Consequently, the PSBR has been large, despite cutbacks in the public sector and higher North Sea oil revenue. The monetarist rowing boat has hardly stayed where it started, let alone made headway. It is difficult to judge whether the fall in inflation rates is primarily the result of depressed economic activity or of government monetary policy. In so far as it is possible to discriminate between the two, my judgement would be in favour of the former. The overall lesson is obvious. The primacy given to money and price movements within the monetarist framework is not justified. They are part of an integrated and complex economy and not the fulcrum of all economic change. Living in the City may produce this rather myopic vision, but the Square Mile is a rather restricted environment.

But the underlying problem remains the belief in naturalism,

31

the competitive market system which is self-regulating and which will sort out our problems if we leave it alone and do not distort it. Monetarists have made themselves priests and prophets within this dogmatic system. This position is false and somewhat disingenuous, since the 'self-regulating' system is actually run by the people who support the Party which supports the policy . . . If money and prices are not the determinants of a self-regulating economic system, and if we are responsible for the way in which markets operate, we would do well to break out of this dogma and recognize that monetary constraint is merely one of the normative issues in the operation of markets. There are many other structural and strategic considerations which must be examined.

Notes

1. There are many variants of monetarism which are all subsumed in the description under a fairly popular version which has most affected the policy of the 1980s Conservative Government. See J. Fleming, *Catch '76* (IEA 1976) and P. Minford, *Is Monetarism Enough?* (IEA 1980). Despite the significant differences all these positions have a similar paradigmatic base.
2. Hayek, Von Mises, Friedman, Gilder and others have provided the ideological justification of this position. It is interesting how heavily British monetarists depend on these Austrian and American sources.
3. A. Storkey, 'The Assumption of the Independence of Supply and Demand Schedules and Market Strategy', Calvin Economics Faculty, 9 October 1980.
4. Price theory moves into this position by using rates of substitution to create price relativities which are held to be objective. All the actual problems of valuation can then be ignored. When money enters into the picture, problems in its valuation are similarly ignored. The determinate price solutions are then found, and money has to be treated as a quasi-independent system. Monetarism is therefore a product of neo-classical price theory.
5. ibid.
6. The point here is more radical, for example, than that made in Hicks' Fixprice model. There Hicks recognizes that equilibrium prices may not obtain and the determination of prices is taken right outside the model. As a result prices, using a *ceteris paribus* framework, are assumed to be exogenously determined and are therefore treated as fixed. The emphasis then switches to

32

the variations in quantities marketed and the dynamics which follow from this. The argument here is that both the Fixprice and Flexprice methods do not relax the determinate price assumptions enough. See J. Hicks, *Capital and Growth* (Oxford University Press 1965), pp. 76ff.

7. In other words traditional monopolistic theory may substantially underestimate the scope that companies and other organizations have for a price rising strategy. In some areas, where overseas competition is available, the scope may be limited, but in many areas it is considerable.

8. Perhaps the most consistent work within the framework of an egocentric utility calculus is that done by Becker. He, too, attempts to incorporate altruism within this framework and comes up with the conclusion that egoists have an incentive to maximize overall income in order to get transfers from the altruist. He even discovers perfectly simulated altruistic behaviour. The sadness of this small egocentric world is evident when marriage, friendship, having children and swopping mates are analysed in these terms. G. Becker, *The Economic Approach to Human Behavior* (University of Chicago Press 1976) and *A Treatise on the Family* (Harvard University Press 1981).

3: The Keynesian Steering Wheel

The Economics of Keynes

In the 1920s and 1930s Keynes was struggling against orthodox ideas to develop a new attack on the desperate unemployment of the inter-war years. Then, as now, there was a widespread defeatism. Nothing could be done other than to wait for natural forces to establish a healthy equilibrium of employment. However, Keynes reinterpreted this equilibrium as a special case of what he believed was a more general model, a pattern where income and expenditure could settle down into stability at levels which corresponded to either heavy unemployment or excess demand for labour. Keynes broke with the idea that the labour market operated naturally on the basis of price calculations. Often prices did not respond in the way they were supposed to. Wages were established by various conventions and refused to show normal market responses, and the employment of workers often depended more heavily on the level of activity in the economy than on response to the market wage rate. More decisive were the flows of income and expenditure generated by the decisions of various groups within the economy. Especially important were the decisions which people made to save, consume and invest. In particular, if people failed to consume and invest sufficiently, the economy could be trapped in a downward spiral of expenditure, which would leave people unable to act as they had earlier intended and could mean many finishing up without jobs. Suddenly here was an actual explanation of unemployment which opened up the possibility of doing something constructive.

This was not just a new theory, but a fundamental break with the 'invisible hand' view of economics, for Keynes showed that the pursuit of individual self-interest could in certain circumstances lead not to automatic good, but to a vicious circle of disaster. The naive optimism of naturalistic economics was shattered not just by circumstances but by real theory! In its place was a model or paradigm·which was not easy to grasp in the old terms. One way in which it was different was the approach to decision-making. Earlier economists saw it as an abstract rational process made on the basis of comprehensive knowledge of the situation. Keynes focused on the institutional setting, limited knowledge, and the actual concerns of the decision makers. He showed that often people have a very limited understanding of what they are doing.

Another difference was Keynes's belief in normative economics. That is, he believed the discipline was centrally concerned with what *should* be done, and should not relegate normative questions to consideration only after 'proper' economic analysis had been completed. He therefore disagreed profoundly with the position of Robbins that economics was a value-free science from which all normative issues were excluded *a priori*.[1] It was of no surprise to him when he built his tank and found it pointing in a different direction. It was also evident to him that his tank could be steered by, for example, the government intervening to maintain the level of domestic demand. It would be right and beneficial, taunted Keynes, to do something completely unnatural like burying banknotes in bottles in the ground for people to dig up to help encourage demand and thereby expand employment.[2] The decisions to consume and invest shape the level of income, and saving is a mere residual, therefore the government should act to encourage the right level of consumption and investment. With the publication of the Beveridge Report in 1944 the government was invited to put its hands firmly to the wheel.[3]

Full Employment in a Free Society, which followed it, was a remarkable document. It asserted the bold theme of its title. Alongside the plan for Social Security which would protect people from the worst terrors of unemployment, illness and old age, Beveridge set forward a policy for employment. The key to the policy was that of maintaining adequate demand, but he was quite clear that there were other necessary moves like controlled location of industry and the increased mobility of labour. The policy was normatively driven. So that we can feel the difference between this approach to economics and the value-free naturalism of most subsequent analysis, let us listen to Beveridge's emphasis:

Whether we can do this, depends upon the degree to which social conscience becomes the driving force of our national life. We should regard Want, Disease, Ignorance and Squalor as common enemies with whom each individual may not seek a separate peace, escaping himself to personal prosperity while leaving his fellows in their clutches. That is the meaning of social conscience; that one should refuse to make a separate peace with social evil. Social conscience, when the barbarous tyranny abroad has ended, should drive us to take up different arms in a new war against Want, Disease, Ignorance and Squalor at home.[4]

The moral thrust of this message is clear. It had a profound effect on post-war economic policy, not just during the periods of the Labour governments. Macmillan, Butler and other leading Conservatives had faced the issue in the 1930s and had moved away from *laissez-faire* minimal government to a more responsible, involved model of how the government should operate. The myopic processes which created unemployment could, they believed, be reversed.

The Debate on Keynes
Since Hicks's *Mr Keynes and the 'Classics': A Suggested Interpretation,* economists have been in the business of reinterpreting Keynes.[5] Many of these presentations have been concerned to show that Keynes was not really so different from his classical predecessors. Especially since the publication of Leijonhufvud's book, *On Keynesian Economics and the Economics of Keynes*,[6] there has been much debate on whether this was the case, and rightly so, for it is important. Either, as Keynes himself felt and said, there is a pattern of thinking which developed in the classics from which it was very difficult to escape, or conventional economics can include a wide variety of opinions and has expressed many similar to those of Keynes both before and after he wrote *The General Theory on Unemployment, Interest and Money*. It is not just a local academic disagreement but of crucial importance to the way in which unemployment is faced. The classical and neo-classical economists thought and think that there is nothing seriously wrong with the way they do economics. There may be a weakness here and there, but modifications can be incorporated into the system of

37

thought which is basically well thought through and incontrovertible. On this view, whatever Keynes said was radically different about his approach could be absorbed, like grit in an oyster shell, into neo-classical economics. The alternative view, accepted by this author, is that the underlying paradigm of classical economics was, and remains, fundamentally flawed. Which is correct?

There was no doubt that Keynes was an irritant. He served in the Treasury during the First World War and attended the post-war Peace Conference at Paris as Deputy for the Chancellor of the Exchequer. He outrightly disagreed with the peace that Lloyd George, Wilson and Clemenceau concluded, and his statements to that effect meant that he quickly resigned.[7] Of course, the meanness of the Peace Treaty did help create the economic depression and nationalism which fuelled the Second World War. The irritant had the effrontery to be right. This at least suggests that we should take Keynes's own feeling of what he was fighting against with some seriousness. What was he opposing? The classical economists believed the economy would naturally tend to an equilibrium, which would in due time eliminate unemployment. If we go for the core of what Keynes was fighting, it was naturalistic economics. This approach was wrongly based and also inaccurate. As Keynes said,

There would obviously be a natural tendency towards the optimum employment of resources in a Society which was functioning after the manner of the classical postulates. It may well be that the classical theory represents the way in which we should like our Economy to behave. But to assume that it actually does so is to assume our difficulty away.[8]

Keynes's model does not need to be defended in all its details, but the change in paradigm which it involved needs to be taken very seriously, for the normative, disequilibrium, decision-centred approach was distinctive.

The New 'Keynesian' Equilibrium
During the 1950s and 1960s a process continued which had got underway soon after Keynes had produced his work. The details of his theory were rebuilt in terms of the old naturalistic view. An income equilibrium model which

operated in largely mechanical ways was developed with an increasing emphasis on various abstract functional relationships. Uncertainty largely disappeared, and decision making moved back into the old rational framework. Samuelson and others developed standardized ways of handling income flows, and few economists were really aware of how different this self-confident Keynesianism was from the work of Keynes himself. Soon Keynesianism was providing naturalistic answers to the problems of the economy. Basically, when unemployment threatened, the economy had to be pumped up again by decreased taxation or increased government expenditure to its full employment level. Solving unemployment was no more difficult than keeping the bath water topped up.

Then, however, the Keynesian theoretical framework developed its own internal problems which are interesting in what they reveal about the naturalistic paradigm. There were now two neat systems of equilibrium analysis on the table: the first was the old money equilibrium, and the second the Keynesian income equilibrium. Both tended within the naturalist framework to be determinate, so there was a tendency for the overall analysis to be overdetermined, or to fall back into two parts. This problem recurs in the literature of the 1960s and 1970s.[9] Further, because of the models' presumed equilibrium, they were often involved in a circularity of argument—it might be necessary to already know the level of income to determine the rate of interest and vice versa. This pattern was justified by using heavily the distinction between statics and dynamics. Statics was the pattern of analysis which could be coped with in terms of yielding a 'natural' equilibrium solution. Dynamics was everything which could not be contained within this logically ordered world. A realistic assessment of the period would conclude that the relationship between statics and dynamics was a tortured one. However, despite these problems, the Keynesian models increased in sophistication and assurance. They provided, it seemed, a total working model of 'the tank' together with a steering wheel. Let us look for a moment at this steering wheel.

The Keynesians believed with some confidence that they had a new grasp of how the 'tank' worked. They understood the mechanism and economic theory became identified with building models of it. Gradually the old naturalistic conception of the economy had reasserted itself through the thinking of Hansen, Samuelson, Hicks and others, with the limited change that the steering wheel was in place and could be used by the government. Political parties had the key role of claiming that they were the people who could use the steering wheel with expertise. A certain technical solution to the problem of how the economy should be steered was the basis of an appeal to the voters, and governments were expected almost magically to deliver full employment on the basis of the Keynesian solution. However, the economy gradually started taking off in directions other than those in which it was steered, and sometimes the 'tank' even seemed to be changing shape. As a result, this secure pattern of under-standing was brought into question. The most obvious problem was the combination of a high level of unemployment with a high level of inflation. Clearly, there was something wrong with the old optimistic Keynesian model. What was it?

A Critique of the Keynesian Model
The monetarists mounted the strongest critique of Keynesianism, and there was obviously some substance to their points. They argued that the expansion of demand carried out through government expenditure had other consequences, whether done through an increase in government borrowing or an expansion of the money supply. The result had to be a higher proportion of national income channelled through the public sector, which meant a decline in private investment and enterprise and an increase in dependent employment (jobs which relied on wealth generated elsewhere in the economy). They also argued, as we have discussed already, that the expansion in the money supply created illusions which prevented markets from operating properly. We can accept these points as important without accepting where they come from, namely the old naturalistic market model which we considered in the previous chapter. But is there another basis for understanding the problems raised by Keynesianism?

Perhaps it can be found in the fact that the Keynesian model is largely pre-institutional and non-normative. There is

40

nothing wrong with examining income flows carefully, but if we look more closely at the Keynesian framework, we see that it focused largely on the public flows and ignored the differences which the institutional context made to those flows. For example, it analysed how family income is channelled into consumption and saving. But what the family is like profoundly affects what that flow will be. If there is a norm that the children will look after aged parents, then there will probably be less saving than if it is assumed one saves for old age. If both spouses are working, and they have relatively little time to spend their money, then it is likely that more will be saved, by default. If families are small, then far less working time is invested in child-rearing and more is available for paid work. All of these institutional dynamics clearly have a deep effect on income flows and possible levels of unemployment. Unless, therefore, the significance of institutions is incorporated into the analysis of income flows, it is likely to remain fundamentally flawed.

This point needs to be pressed further. The concentration on public flows meant that income flows *within* organizations and institutions were largely ignored, with the exception of government. However, it is now becoming evident that vast amounts of income move within firms, banks, families, central and local government and multinational companies in ways which radically affect the development of the economy. Just because these movements are often treated very secretively and little information is available about many of them, does not mean they can be ignored. At an elementary level the point is obvious. When a firm moves capital and jobs from one area of the country to another, it obviously has a profound effect on patterns of income even though it is largely an internal transaction. When the central government, through rate-capping or whatever, changes the distribution of grants to local authorities, people and their jobs experience the change. When multinationals or banks move money abroad within their own organizations the patterns of investment in Britain are changed and people's jobs are affected.

Another criticism concerns the relationship between flows of income and wealth. When Keynes was writing, most of the population had very little wealth in relation to their annual income. They were living, so to speak, hand to mouth, and their consumption and saving were therefore most closely related to income. Over the last fifty years there have been massive changes in this area. Families, along with other institutions like unions, pension funds, companies, banks, local authorities have become substantial holders of wealth. The ratio between family wealth and family income has moved from something like 1:1 to 5:1 over that period. Thus, many families are able to be much more discretionary and strategic in their financial decisions. This requires the analysis of the effects of wealth and of the strategic policies families and other institutions pursue in relation to it. As we saw in the previous chapter the area of normative discretion in the markets for wealth is potentially very great and must be taken into account.

But this in turn requires examination of the normative direction of institutional policy, and here we meet the malaise of Keynesian thinking. Nobody other than the government is responsible for unemployment. The 'tank' moves on, and when it begins to misbehave and to perform erratically everybody waits for the government to do something about it. When the government complains that the steering is faulty, people shrug their shoulders, and eventually when the Conservative Government declares that it is going to get out of the driving seat and leave the 'tank' to drive itself, they are very understanding and ask what else can be done? To recognize the contribution of unions, banks, central and local government, firms, families and financial institutions to the generation and growth of unemployment is not possible when the economy is seen as a glorious flow chart of functional relationships which are in equilibrium.

The Institutional Degeneration of the British Economy
However, it is not merely a question of criticizing the Keynesian position. For when it became the dominant ideology, there was a general abdication of wider responsibility and a consensus for self-interested *laissez-faire* in institutional life, even among those on the Left. Particularly, there was a deterioration in the norms of institutional life. The list is a depressing one, but we should face it, especially because it points to the danger of the underlying malaise: 'The economy is not our responsibility. Our task is to make

sure that we defend our own interests.' This attitude dominated institutional development.

Firms exhibited a lower commitment to serving the consumer with their products. Quality, delivery times, back-up and service deteriorated. The long-term commitment through research and development to improving the product for the consumer was not taken seriously, despite fine educational preparation for this kind of work. There was a reliance on customers who purchased by custom, rather than a concern to identify new ones and expand sales. Consumers were often given what the firm thought they needed, rather than a real attempt being made to find out what their needs actually were. During periods of high demand the customer was forced to pay by queueing or higher prices, rather than helped through forethought and committed production. Often firms were not even aware of new emerging markets, whether in small motorbikes or transistor radios, because they were so out of touch with the consumers.

The attitude to the workers was no better. While Germany was practising co-partnership with the workers at the highest level within the company, and the Japanese were opening up close working relationships between managers and other workers, the British remained stiffly adversarial. The main ambition of the managers seemed to be to keep the workers in their place and to minimize the exercise of responsibility and maximize passivity. Any growth in the prosperity of a company was immediately the scene of a squabble between profits and wages as to who should get the most. Secrecy and lack of information characterized the relationship between the two adversarial groups. Each through its respective political allies sought policies which gave it an advantage over the other. Many attitudes to work were destructive, unco-operative and ritualized with petty rows over rules and job demarcation.

The same selfishness was also evident within government. It was not coincidental that the three election years of the Conservative Government's period in office, in 1955, 1959 and 1964 occurred in periods of Keynesian-generated boom, accompanied in 1959 by the slogan 'You've never had it so good'. This manipulation of the electorate, shoving prosperity temporarily under its nose so that it will vote Tory, which misfired slightly in 1964, also had a bad effect on the economy. It induced firms to hire and fire workers to cope with the fluctuations in output rather than undertaking long-term capital investment. It also led to shortage-induced imports flooding in during certain periods and getting a good introduction to British markets. The regular financial crises and interest rate fluctuations also conspired against careful long-term planning.

When the Labour Government came to power in 1964 it was committed to national indicative planning which we shall examine more fully in the next chapter. This involved increasing regulation and direction of industry. Industrial relations became an absorbing activity of the State, and planning as conceived by Harold Wilson and George Brown became the key to policy, although it had collapsed by the late 1960s. What followed initially under the new Conservative Government was another change in direction (reflecting the way in which the adversarial voting system has played havoc with economic policy). But then this Government, at least by 1972, was pursuing a consistent Keynesian policy. It hoped that a rapid expansion in demand would induce higher levels of output and investment so that Britain would take off into a higher level of growth. In terms of an immediate attack on unemployment it was quite successful, but it ran into problems of foreign trade deficits and the confrontation between the miners and the Government.

Again there was a change of government and policy. This time the concern was institutional, but not in terms of institutional reform. Government policy focused on the establishment of peaceful relationships between the status quo unions and government. It also met with traditional Keynesian tools the trade crises which acted as a restraint on any further expansion of the economy. Five years later there was another major change in government policy to the monetarism of the Thatcher governments. Our concern at present is not for the policies of these governments, but on what they have done with the institutions of government which are most concerned with economic affairs. Policy changes have prevented a responsible growth in these institutions. They have been created, disbanded, changed, merged and eliminated. Few, for example, will now remember the Industrial Reorganization Corporation. It was created in 1966, manned by experienced people committed to private enterprise, and its task was to advise and help companies in reorganization. It could borrow funds from the public sector, and earn returns on them, and by the late 1960s it was paying the Treasury a dividend of £500,000 or more. With a change of government this organization was scuppered.[10] This pattern has been repeated so often, with the additional merry-go-round of nationalization and denationalization, that it cannot but have severely damaged the development of the British economy.

Nor is it only the large institutions which have been part of this decay. Families and schools exhibit the same pattern. Consider, for example, the area of vandalism, crime and security. The costs in these areas have soared since the 1960s. Indeed, the only orthodox attitude to these problem areas is that we will pay to protect ourselves from them on the basis of self-interest. So protection and security have become one of the few modern growth industries and the police find themselves increasingly in the role of handling widespread social breakdown. But this policy of paying our way out of areas of personal and family failure is a gigantic mistake. The costs of security soar, but with no real benefits. Crime becomes endemic in new areas as the communities decay and their populations become bitter and desperate. Pressures on medical services, preventive agencies, social workers, the prisons and schools mount. All of this costs billions, with nothing of benefit to the community to show for the expenditure. Indeed, all there is to show for it is broken lives and failure.

This institutional failure slips through the net of Keynesian analysis and policy. The technical, mechanical framework just cannot take it into account. Its prescriptions assume that people are automata, rather than acknowledging their full personhood. This is not just an abstract mistake, but a view which is daily costing us millions. The poverty of the debate between the major parties on institutional reform is summarized in the polar positions they normally adopt. Either abolish as much as possible in the public sector, and things will *automatically* get better, or rescue institutions from the clutches of private greedy men and women by bringing them

45

into the public sector, and things will similarly improve. As a result of this dreary deadlock debate, institutional reform is ignored and postponed. Although a majority of the electorate has accepted the arguments for electoral reform during the 1970s and 1980s, the major parties have dismissed them as irrelevant. In the same way other reforms are ignored unless they fit with the sterile debate outlined above, when they become little more than the trading of empty eggshells.

Keynesianism and Wealth

It has already been suggested that the Keynesian framework has ignored the significance of wealth in contemporary economic activity. But this point needs to be pushed further. Wealth is important in a number of ways. First, it increases the discretion of the decision makers. Second, the distribution of wealth has a profound effect on the way the macroeconomic flows of income are channelled. Third, the value of wealth is widely problematic in a way which creates questions about valuation throughout the economy. Let us examine each of these in turn.

Discretion, as we have already suggested, is highly important. Let us consider for a moment the distinction between consumption and investment, basic to conventional macroeconomics. 'Consumption' as a concept depends on the idea that people have to buy it to survive. Sometimes the concept is seen in terms of items being used up instantly, but both the calcium in our bones and 'consumer durables' suggest this approach is not definitive. The substantial point is that decision makers with wealth have such discretion that the distinction between investment and consumption becomes blurred. Most of the decisions have both an immediate and a longer-term significance, and their possible directions become more diverse. Consumption can be delayed for strategic reasons which have a big effect on some markets—the bunching of car demand in the new-registration month of August shows how significant it can be. The focus of demand also affects employment. Say, for example, 'consumers' value old masters more highly than contemporary paintings. This stirs the existing pool of works of art, and redistributes wealth in windfall gains, but apart from providing work for a dealer or two, it does little for those who would earn their living by painting. This example, insignificant in its way, is repeated in far more substantial ways throughout the economy. Keynes could look at largely necessary consumption which had predictable consequences. The Keynesians went through the same mechanical movements, but ignored the changes in the situation. Now we have to take notice of the discretion brought by wealth to institutional decision makers.

But this is not all. It has been a commonplace of Keynesian analysis that the marginal propensity to consume (the proportion of extra income spent) of lower-income families is greater than that of higher-income families. This, in itself, is highly significant in a period where income discrepancies are increasing, but it is only part of the story. It ignores the impact of unequal expenditure of *wealth*, and the kind of expenditure which rich and poor groups are characteristically undertaking. For example, rich holders of funds view a rise in interest rates in mixed ways depending on their main concern: if they want to maximize income from the funds, it is good; if they want to maximize asset value, it is likely to be bad. Poorer people tend to find a rise uniformly bad. Clearly, the two groups have different priorities. There are other important differences. The rich are more likely to spend on high technology (low labour input) goods, to go for already existing, positional assets (with zero labour input), to invest abroad (with zero domestic job creation) and to spend a reduced proportion of current income. Here we are not just talking about rich families, but other wealthy institutions as well. The conclusion which at least invites further examination is that a transfer of funds to the rich leads almost inevitably to a depressed economy.

Indeed, it can be argued that the depressions of the late 1870s and 1880s and those of the 1920s and 1930s had exactly this origin. The transfer of funds to the rich which occurred through the high real interest rates on the First World War National Debt combined with the industrial blight of the North perhaps contributed through depressed demand to the Great Slump as much as the more dramatic Wall Street Crash. Possibly the same process is operating today, when the holding and concentration of discretionary wealth has increased substantially.

There is another development which is potentially more

47

dangerous. It is best described by saying that the kind of disjunction between the 'paper' and 'real' values of wealth which occurred in the United States before 1929 are now normal. The value of wealth is now very ambiguous and fluctuates in normal economic activity more dramatically than at any other period of our recent history. Whether the item of wealth is the dollar, property, land values, shares or government stock, variations in perceived value have had a massive influence on many people's lives and jobs. This pattern is partly the result of the unstable structure of many of our capital markets, but there is another reason. Wealth, as Ruskin so eloquently argued, only has value as it is used.[11] Storing up treasure for ourselves is a powerful, but empty, idea. The value of wealth therefore depends heavily on its usefulness, but as the capital/output ratio grows, any instability in the usefulness is likely to produce much greater instability in the value of wealth. For this and other reasons the valuation of assets is becoming more unstable, and yet changes in these markets are able to deeply affect conventional income flows, especially through decisions and situations (like widespread bankruptcies) which may exist among institutions. On the whole this kind of instability and the overall significance of wealth is ignored within the conventional Keynesian framework.

Normativity and Automatic Keynesianism

The complacency of macroeconomic analysis in the 1960s and 1970s has now bitten the dust. Even those still thinking in terms of maneouvring the 'tank', acknowledge that it is damned cussed. Yet clearly the possibility of expanding the economy through 'Keynesian' policy remains important. How can expansion take place which does not run into the problems encountered in previous attempts?

What we have discussed earlier suggests that income and expenditure flows are very inadequate measures of the wholesome growth of an economy. They do not take into account institutional development, the normative quality of markets, the distribution of flows and the actual benefits which people may or may not receive from goods and services. This means that the real direction of economic development is seen very darkly through the glass of Keynesian analysis. For example, the Government's sale of British Telecom, British Airways and British Gas has stirred up a lot of macroeconomic mud and involves massive private investment in *already existing assets*. What this means in terms of the development of the economy is highly ambiguous. As a consequence we can no longer use these macroeconomic measures as our basic frame of reference. This argument becomes compelling when we recognize that the patterns of transmission of income and expenditure which occur within institutions are completely ignored in the Keynesian framework.

How are these omissions to be corrected? Arguably, at present there is a gap in the areas of information deemed to be significant for policy decisions. On the one hand there has been a long tradition of using the Keynesian macroeconomic indicators of income and expenditure for policy decisions. On the other hand there has been a concern, especially within monetarism, for the micro and macroeconomic indicators of price variations. However, these are also less reliable as indicators of our economic situation than has hitherto been assumed. But the gap in information which remains concerns the income and wealth flows which various institutions experience. For it is here that the basic shape and development of the economy must be plotted. If many families are experiencing windfall gains and others considerable capital losses through movements in the property market, it is important information. If the contraction of demand for various infrastructural companies is leading to work loss, we should know. If government expenditure in certain departments is area-partial, it should be public information. If banks are transmitting funds abroad on a substantial scale, we should know how much and where it is going. The institutional map of the economy is at present very sketchily drawn, and without it we cannot tackle the task of recreating employment.

For our employment goal can now be redefined. It is to increase the flow of income and resources to employing institutions if they will use these to broaden employment. Even sophisticated Keynesian policies 'hope' that flows will generate extra jobs. It is now obvious that in many cases this will not happen unless the institutional structures change.

49

The strategy must explicitly take into account what these structures are and should be like.

This raises the issue of privacy. There is at present a massive conceptual division between public and private, which creates a strong tendency for the private sector to retain information about itself to itself. The Conservative governments of the 1980s actually encouraged this trend by no longer authorizing the collection of information on personal wealth. Public corporations have also cut back significantly on the institutional information which they make available. This conception is absurd. We are talking about vast and significant institutions whose effect on the economy is of great strategic significance. At present many people whose lives are directly bound up in various institutions have little or no idea of their resources and economic situation. This information should be available and should be a vital qualitative guide to public policy. Later chapters will explore in more detail what kind of information and strategic issues need to be opened up.

These are detailed criticisms. There remains a bigger problem. This is the mind-set which dominates much thinking in professional economics. Many economists have taken naturalism on into abstract and mechanical patterns of analysis which are impersonal and deinstitutionalized. Their professional ethos requires that they do so. Yet this work, whether Keynesian in focus or not, fails and does not pretend to address the needs and concerns of the workers and workless. It has used the lamentably weak division between positive and normative to cut itself off from the question of how we should live economically. Since this question is at the heart of our economic problems, it is one we should face.

Notes

1. R. Harrod, *The Life of John Maynard Keynes* (Penguin 2nd edn, reprint of the 1952 edn), p. 253.
2. J. M. Keynes, *The General Theory of Employment, Interest and Money* (Macmillan 1961), pp. 128—31.
3. See Chapter 10.
4. Beveridge, *Full Employment in a Free Society.*
5. *Econometrica*, vol. 5, no. 2 (1937), pp. 147—59.
6. New York, Oxford University Press 1968.

7. J. M. Keynes, *The Economic Consequences of the Peace* (Macmillan 1920), especially pp. 209ff.
8. *General Theory*, pp. 33−4.
9. Addressed by Patinkin especially. See also A. Coddington, *Keynesian Economics* (George Allen and Unwin 1983), pp. 9−23.
10. See S. Young with A. V. Lowe, *Intervention in the Mixed Economy* (Croom Helm 1974).
11. J. Ruskin, *Unto This Last* (George Allen 1900), pp. 38−66, 105−74.

4: The Marxist and Socialist Alternatives

The Marxist Diagnosis
At a number of periods in British economic history there have been profound problems including widespread poverty and unemployment. The naturalistic view of the classical economists resulted in these situations being distanced as a technical failure in the mechanisms of the economy. Yet simply because people were aware things were wrong, they were not able to accept the bland assurances of the classical economists. This pattern occurred in the period before (and during) the First World War, in the 1920s and 1930s, and it is likely to recur in the 1990s and beyond. One of the intriguing questions of history is what would have happened if the answers of Keynes and Beveridge had not been available during and after the Second World War. We assume, because it suits us, that the map of Europe was drawn largely through conquest, but it is also true that at the end of the Second World War the failures of capitalism were manifest, and there were not many answers other than those provided by socialism. If we have to face a situation like the one in 1929, this may well again be the answer. What is the socialist diagnosis and whence its strength?

Although the Marxist and socialist positions need to be distinguished, it is the former which has largely shaped the economic response of socialism and which should be considered first. Marx, drawing on a long tradition which went back into the medieval Church, took a fundamental, bold step which changed the whole way in which unemployment could be approached. The classical economists saw value and prices as being determined by market forces. Marx saw all value as having its origin in labour. The labour theory of value redefined the approach to the issue of employment. If value has its source in labour, then employment is good *per se*, and the economy is therefore organized for work. In other words, before anything else is done, everybody is given a job. The outcome of this position in socialist countries is that,

53

formally at least, there is zero unemployment. Our fundamental problem is solved. How effective the work may be is a subsidiary question. On the face of it this radical move transforms the whole issue and meets a basic weakness in the classical scheme of economics.[1]

For in many of the normal approaches to economic theory consumption is seen as having utility, while work has disutility. It is an unpleasant activity for which the worker is compensated by receiving pay. Now if work is viewed so negatively within the orthodox scheme of things, it is not surprising that somewhere along the way this negatively defined concept should be given a low priority in public policy. Or, to put it another way, if consumption is made the focus of all good in neo-classical economics, then work is likely to become a pawn in the consumer-driven society. Clearly, there is a substantial issue of values here, and it may be that the Marxist focus is an important corrective to this negative view of work.

What is involved in a labour theory of value? It means that nothing has value until *utilized* by workers; only work makes the resources of the environment accessible to human needs. It also means that other supposed sources of value, like capital, must be seen as originating in the complex pattern of labour which has gone into their development. More particularly, it means that the wage paid for work may well not represent its true value. There may be a surplus value which is appropriated by someone other than the worker — the capitalist or the consumer (although this is a less well developed Marxist theme). This theory of surplus value has important consequences for the view of unemployment, for normally Marxists have argued and do argue that unemployment is caused by wages being too low. To some this may seem like a peculiar dogmatism, but it is really no different from the naturalist economists arguing that wages are too high on the basis of a natural equilibrium which exists only in their heads, so we would do well to consider it.

Why are wages too low? They are held down by the ability of capitalists to generate labour-saving capital, to export labour through international colonialism and to create a technology which eliminates labour dependence. All of these succeed in generating a reserve army of labour which guarantees that there will be surplus value which can be appropriated by the owners of capital. Yet when wages are low, other consequences follow. One is an inherent tendency towards underconsumption, since many of the workers are not receiving the resources which would enable them to keep the economy at full production. Another is a tendency to create excessive private capital out of the surplus which raises the productivity of labour and reduces the number of workers necessary. Yet another is the drive of capitalists to transform their surpluses into technological power which can further reduce their dependence on workers. On this view, therefore, unemployment may well have its roots in wages which are too low, both in the home country and especially in the Third World opened up by international capitalism.[2]

These detailed arguments need to be examined further in their own terms, but our main concern is to investigate a paradigm based on the labour theory of value. In fact it turns out to be an extremely dogmatic one, for with labour as the ultimate base of value the position is saying *a priori* that there are no economic problems. Whatever is produced by labour is good, and the whole system needs to be commanded, politically, to work through this premiss. Thus Marxism in most of its varieties becomes profoundly rigid — economic relationships, problems of scarcity and choice, the development of capital, the significance of work and the standard of living are merely technical details once the underlying problem of capitalism is solved and people acknowledge a labour theory of value. It is for this reason that the command economy of Russia and other State Socialist countries fits so well with Marxism, for it says that there are no substantial economic problems, especially of course among the workforce who have been accorded ultimate value. When this value does not seem to be reflected in the political direction of labour, deep dissatisfaction and poor rewards, the dogma is asserted more fiercely over the evidence to the contrary.

Asserting labour as the ultimate value does not work. It ignores the underlying reality that the purpose of work is mutual service. So, rather than labour being an end in itself it needs to be sensitively orientated to those who are being served and to receive messages about the best way to serve. The labour theory of value obliterates all these important relational issues, subsuming them under the centralized control of the work-force, and as a result provides an impoverished awareness of unemployment.

Thus, labour as an idol does not solve our problem of a paradigm. It is certainly an alternative to the naturalist one, but it has its own simplicity and unreality which has the result of impoverishing people's lives, and in practice all kinds of proximate economic techniques have been brought in to cope with the problems generated by this total economic framework.

Marxism and Justice
The positions we have examined thus far have not been concerned with justice. Indeed, the naturalistic model has no place for justice within its terms of reference. As we saw earlier, it involved adopting the onlooker approach with its deliberate detachment and its total absolution from norms. When an issue of justice comes up, the naturalistic economist must, in theory, wring his hands and say, 'There is nothing I can do about it; that's the way the economy *is*'. Fortunately, such people are sometimes better in practice than they are in theory. Keynes challenged this position. The way the market works was not accepted as the last word on the subject. Often, it could fail by its own criteria. But even Keynes challenged the position largely from inside. Beveridge and others brought to the subject a stronger conception of what was right, but the most obvious imperative to justice has come from Marxism.

Marx had, of course, his own version of naturalism,[3] involving the necessary and ultimate triumph of the proletariat, but fused into his teaching on socialism was the normative judgement that the capitalist classes were unjust to the working classes. This moved outside the naturalist framework (although many Marxists and socialists succeeded in tangling themselves in naturalist dialectics for ever) because it faced the issue of relationships, rather than the classical obsession with people and things. Moreover, Marx had the temerity to suggest that the explanations given for economic and other events might be ideological justifications of what the capitalist classes had unjustly done. The actual terms in which Marx and his followers approached the issue of justice was always through the concept of class. It was, in effect, the only relationship around which issues of justice could cluster. The classical economists had said wages were automatically tied to the value of the worker's output. The Marxists said that over and above the wages paid there was surplus value unfairly appropriated by the capitalists. The counter-assertion exposed the dogma of the classical position, and in some periods was a more compelling one. The affluent houses, servants and conspicuous wealth made it obvious that the capitalists had obtained surpluses, probably unfairly.

When the theme of class injustice was brought to bear on the issue of unemployment, other conclusions followed. The first and most important was the interest capitalists have in high levels of unemployment because of the power it confers on them to hold down wages, weaken unions and create competition among workers. The second was the way firms with some kind of monopoly situation are likely to operate at a lower level of output and employment than that which is most efficient in terms of costs. Third, there was the recognition that international capital could transport jobs overseas to exploit cheaper labour. There were also a number of arguments suggesting ways in which capitalism might be an unstable system. The net effect of these instabilities could be, it was argued, the creation of massive unemployment as a result of practices which were unfair to the workers. In the 1930s the close relationship between unemployment and the failure of capitalism was all too evident.

None of these arguments is likely to lose conviction during the 1990s. Certainly, they should not be dismissed, as they often are by naturalist economists within whose framework these points have no meaning. However, we can still legitimately ask whether this is an adequate view of justice? Here we get an answer which is less than satisfactory. Marx himself was committed to a form of historicism, a belief that the breakdown of capitalism was historically inevitable in the nature of things. This emphasis in Marxism is fundamentally anormative and provides no basis upon which an awareness of justice can be developed. Rather than being an analysis which aims to get to the convoluted guts of what is wrong and unjust, it ends up by being triumphalist. Marx also was deeply affected by the naturalistic economics of Smith and

57

Ricardo. This meant that he too was tied to analysis in terms of determinate forces from which the significance of moral responsibilities had been squeezed out. Although he had some Jewish prophetic fervour in his veins, Marx really had no adequate basis for understanding justice.

An even greater problem was the insistence upon class as the root category for considering justice. Capitalists as a class are the source of injustice and unemployment. It is possible to argue that, in the mid nineteenth century during a *laissez-faire* enterprise-dominated era, capitalists had the greatest economic discretion for justice or injustice. Now, without question, there are many other groups which have a strategic role in the economy—financiers, unions, government, the Treasury, banks and consumers. All of these groups, and potentially many others, have the scope for injustice, and to fix the issue of injustice arbitrarily in capitalism is simply to blinker the whole of one's analysis. Yet this is what Marxism has done. It has become a position which attacks one stronghold to some extent irrespective of whether the enemy is located there or not. This focus of attack reflects the critique's origin. The working class is necessarily outside the analysis. It is always the group which is sinned against. Thus wage increases are always an attempt to recover ground from the overfed shareholders and cannot be seen in other frames of analysis which might show them to be wrong in exploiting other groups. Similarly, the loss of jobs can never be seen as the result of parasitic patterns of work and a failure to respond responsibly to the challenges of the job. The absence of reflexive criticism leaves this position with a soft underbelly. There can be nothing wrong with the workers who are always seen as the fodder of their masters. This argument reflects a very powerful rhetoric in socialism and the thinking of the party which most closely espouses it. The underlying question it raises is whether any ideology which grounds its concept of justice in the righteousness of one group can meet our needs.

The State and Salvation

Can State activity save the economy? This was no great theme of Marx's work but it has become the cornerstone of socialist orthodoxy. In part this is because the labour theory of value requires a total and extra-economic solution, and in part historically it was through the import of paternalist statist ideas from Bismarck's Germany into the thinking of the Labour Party. As Thompson shows, modern British socialism does not draw its statist thinking from the older radical patterns.[4] Statism is such a deeply held tenet of belief, fostered as well by the Conservative Party as the Labour, that it needs to be taken very seriously.[5] Can the State solve unemployment? There have been many programmes over the years which have implicitly seen the State as this kind of agent of salvation. Keynesianism gave the State this role. The vision has often been embodied in a belief in central planning; this idea was pursued in post-war nationalization in the era of Cripps. In the 1960s another version came to grief when George Brown, the Department of Economic Affairs and the National Economic Development Council proved unable to develop indicative planning as a way of leading the economy to success. In the 1970s it was hoped that a concordat between the government and the unions would provide the basis for stable, planned, national economic growth. Again it proved a shell which soon cracked.

At the risk of parodying this point of view it is worth describing the central conception when the socialist State intervenes in the economy. The economy is still seen in naturalistic terms, but it is no longer the benign and beneficent machine of the monetarists; rather, it is a chaos of often destructive behaviour which needs ordering and controlling. There is, of course, an appeal in seeing the seething mass of egocentric behaviour which naturalist economics venerates as a chaos. Yet at the same time it is a fundamentally destructive view, because it means dismissing the norms and responsibility which shape personal and institutional economic life and focusing all responsibility in the State. As a result there is no inner point of contact with what financiers, managers, salesmen, shareholders and others are responsible for doing. The stance is one of external control of economic chaos.

This position is reflected in one of the most tired and useless debates of British public life. Like a fiddler's elbow the debate of freedom and control saws away with naturalistic freedom on the upbeat and antichaotic control on the downbeat. Every British citizen knows the tunes by heart and knows instinctively that expressed in those terms they will get nowhere. Faith in control is as degenerate an economic response as the idea of self-referential freedom. Neither recognizes and responds to the meaning of economic life in a fuller sense. Nevertheless the see-saw goes on. Nationalization, denationalization, renationalization and privatization wearily succeed one another. Control, freedom, planning, initiative, centralized decision making and bureaucracy appear and disappear as political terms. They *may* reflect a false and worn-out antithesis which needs rejecting at a more fundamental level.

But the issue is going to return with more urgency in the form of the question: Can the State provide jobs? This is not just a question for socialists. The Conservative Government in the mid 1980s was providing nearly a million jobs and had therefore also entered into this way of viewing things. They should at least have asked themselves how they became committed to this fundamental compromise of their own principles. Clearly, the State can provide jobs, for example to the young, but what is wrong with this process? If jobs are merely to provide the young with the label of being employed, then the inner meaning of work is compromised. The young are being patronized, fobbed off and found things to do. This does not mean that Youth Training Schemes should not be operated, but they are not likely to develop economic integrity in a deeper sense. They are relieving symptoms, not meeting the underlying needs. It may be that the weakness of *laissez-faire* Conservatism has something to do with this need to compromise.

The issue of whether the State can provide jobs is related to the size of the public sector as an economic agent. This again is part of the old debate, and it is worth rehearsing the two positions. The socialist view sees the government as a source of economic dynamic which can mobilize funds and resources and use them in socially constructive and job-constructive ways. Governments can act faster than markets — to stimulate housebuilding or corporate investment, or directly make jobs. As the example of Sweden shows, it is possible to have a very high proportion of publicly controlled activity with prosperity and growth. No, counter the

60

Conservatives. The growth of the public sector means that a bloated public sector is parasitically feeding through taxes on the dynamic private sector which is actually involved in wealth creation. 'Crowding out' means that higher public-sector expenditure decreases private expenditure, especially private investment through high interest rates and other changes. Lack of accountability in the public sector also leads to widespread inefficiency. On the contrary, counters the Labour Party, it is dynamic public-sector companies like British Airways, British Telecom, the British National Oil Corporation and British Petroleum which have been sold off and avidly bought by Conservatives. Clearly, the argument can go on for a long while. What both positions ignore is the quality and development of the institutions which comprise the public or private sector. This is the crucial issue for all of us.

There is another development which has also compromised the position of socialists believing in State activity. As the public sector has expanded, it has largely been manned by professional and middle-class people who have possibly proved more adept at establishing their own position than at carrying out the transformations which some socialists have had in mind. In terms of its personnel, practices and priorities the public sector has sometimes actually pursued policies at odds with the provision of welfare, improvements in labour policy and other goals of the Left. Instead it has pursued policies which are self-serving and seem to have less penetrative power to touch social ills. In this sense, too, the institution which socialists put their faith in has let them down.[6]

Belief in the State as the instrument for transforming the economy has obviously taken a battering. It is no longer easy to define the State's economic role as that of controller or central planner, and in contemporary socialism it is not easy to see what the definitive economic purpose of the State is. Certainly this is one of the major issues which remains unresolved in the current situation.

Conclusion

We have examined briefly whether Marxism and socialism provide an alternative paradigm to the naturalist one for addressing the issue of employment, and if the above arguments are correct, it seems that they do not. The labour theory of value asserts a solution, but the total assertion turns out to give little detailed guidance. Indeed, the concepts of economic justice associated with this viewpoint fail to give relevant contemporary direction to our policies. Finally, we have seen that the hope vested in the State as the instrument to solve unemployment has for reasons of inner logic been historically disappointed.

Where does this leave us? Possibly with a deepened sense of pessimism. If the preceeding analysis is correct there are major disagreements about the way in which unemployment should be tackled economically and politically. Moreover, people in the various positions disagree about what they disagree about. At the same time each of the main positions we have examined has substantial internal problems and has failed in important respects when carried through. In this context the fatalism we examined at the start of this book seems entirely justified. But we are not quite back to the beginning. For we have seen how deeply rooted this failure is in the naturalism of the Enlightenment, even in the case of Marxism. It may be that a firm break from this paradigm will enable us to consider other possibilities which have hitherto been largely excluded from the debate.

Already some of the old rigidities have broken down. The naturalistic distinction between positive and normative can be finally buried. The almost mystical worship of and description of the market as an ultimate reality can be thrown away. The polarization between public and private has proved a hollow conceptualization. The distinction between micro and macroeconomics has been bridged by a greater institutional awareness, and the identification of work with disutility has been replaced by a more positive evaluation. But these bits and pieces, important though they are, are insignificant besides the deeper issue which is at stake.

That which people worship becomes their master. Gradually over the decades the economy, and its special form of knowledge, have been granted autonomy. Faith has been vested in the market, the power of money, economic progress, patterns of manipulation and the automative benefits of materialism. Economists who have declared themselves pure and unstained by any faith have been tacitly bowing down to these masters. The idols have failed. We have bowed down before the idols we have made and now they laugh at us. How silly to worship markets when they are our handiwork. How pathetic to treat the State as some kind of magical solution. How vain to vest in the bits of paper which we have created the control of our economic policy. The rest of this book takes up the uncomfortable task of recognizing our responsibility before God for our economic lives and the lives of our neighbours, especially the unemployed ones.[7]

Notes

1. Worked through by Marx, especially in *Grundrisse* (Pelican 1973), pp. 557ff.
2. For a fully articulated presentation of a similar position, see E. Mandel, *Marxist Economic Theory*, vols. i and ii (Merlin Press 1971) and *Late Capitalism* (Verso 1978).
3. Marx's naturalism had three different strands: the rationalist naturalism of Ricardian economics, the historicism of mid-nineteenth-century German thinking and the materialist reaction to Hegel. Each in its way had no integral concept of justice.
4. E. P. Thompson, *The Making of the English Working Class* (Penguin 1968), especially the warning about reading back Welfare State socialism into the early nineteenth century, pp. 12—13.
5. Conservative centralism focuses on the one-nation theme, the need for a directing élite and a benevolent but limited paternalism.
6. A. Storkey, *A Christian Social Perspective* (IVP 1979), pp. 179—85.
7. See B. Goudzwaard, *Idols of our Time* (IVP 1984).

PART TWO
THE ALTERNATIVE
CHRISTIAN PARADIGM

This part addresses the issue of providing an alternative approach to the problem of unemployment. In the first chapter some of the key elements of this new approach are built up, often with contrasting comparisons to the current ways of doing things. The implications of a Christian view of responsibility and of economic relationships are developed. Then the organizing principle of this whole section is outlined. In the modern economy, economic discretion—the source of the important developments in the economy—lies with economic institutions. These therefore should be the main focus of economic analysis, not the often mechanical and pedestrian transactions which are normally examined. The first chapter opens up a Christian understanding of institutions and structural principles as an introduction to the detailed analysis of later chapters. It then looks at other elements in a Christian paradigm and specifically focuses on the meaning of work and the central Christian response to unemployment.

The emphasis in the following chapters is upon how institutions may be contributing to the growth in unemployment. The structural principles by which they do and should operate are considered, and it emerges that in many institutions there are internal pressures which generate unemployment and which prevent the problem from being addressed in a constructive way. Contrary to the orthodox suppositions, institutions like the family, banks, professions and companies have a profound effect on employment in the economy. It becomes clear that underconsumption, poor investment, poor distribution of labour, under-utilization of resources, inflation and other major contributors to unemployment can be identified and understood in institutional terms.

But this is not just another technical analysis, this time of institutions, for it also shows that many of these failures are failures of norms and principles governing our economic activity. Many of these situations are unfair to those who are vulnerable in our economy, raising the issue of establishing more just economic relationships. What emerges through these chapters is a detailed map of the way this 'insoluble' problem is actually generated by our decisions and behaviour. We therefore have the power to put things right. This will be the theme of Part Three.

5:   A Christian Paradigm

Apologia for a Christian Way

A conclusion which can be drawn from the preceding discussion is that the Enlightenment way of doing economics has left us without a coherent response to our problems. Many other economists have noticed the jangle of opinions. Blaug summed up the situation thus in 1980:

The 1960s was a decade in which the public esteem of economics rose to an all-time pitch. The 1970s, on the other hand, have been full of talk of 'crisis', 'revolution', and 'counter-revolution', amounting at times to a veritable orgy of self-criticism on the part of some of the leading spokesmen of the economics profession.[1]

In the subsequent period the discipline has experienced something like a pitched battle between the monetarists and the non-monetarists and things have got worse. The discipline is incoherent in at least one sense of the word. But it is not just the integrity of the discipline which is at stake. On a longer time scale, orthodoxy has a more serious case to answer than that of squabbling. Orthodox economics, it can be argued, has rolled on nicely when there were not too many problems around, because it did not matter too much what was being said anyway, but during the late nineteenth century, the inter-war period and presently, when problems became acute, it has proved bankrupt. Other non-orthodox movements like Victorian moral concern, socialism and the work of Keynes were needed to fill in the vacuum of constructive help. In so far as this charge is justified, it suggests that we might do well to consider a Christian alternative to the naturalistic economics of the Enlightenment.

To some people, of course, the idea is unthinkable. After all there is knowledge which is objective, scientific and reliable, and faith which is subjective and private. Sadly, however, the arguments by which knowledge was held to be objective and scientific are now looking rather the worse for wear. The idea of factual, empirical knowledge has been shown to be a delusion; there are always prior patterns of interpretation which compromise the so-called 'objectivity' of the facts.

Rational understanding can be bought in many decidely different supermarkets. Logic is either an empty tautology or is biased in a certain direction. The study of human behaviour becomes the manipulation of human beings by pigeons who are out for a healthy diet. All the supposedly certain routes to human knowledge have turned out to be cul-de-sacs.[2]

The other side of this dog-eared division is no less suspect. Shunting Christian understanding off into the area of subjective faith is one of the ways of trying to maintain that knowledge can be made independent of faith. However, it is now becoming inescapably clear that all knowledge necessarily involves commitments of faith and belief.[3] Far from being private, Christian knowledge has always been public, public enough to be based on the Creator's knowledge of the whole of the creation. It is knowledge in the deeper sense that we are known by God better than we know ourselves, personally, socially, economically and historically. The Christian message involves questioning whether we know as much as we think we do, whether faith in reason, science, human experience, facts and logic can produce the indubitable knowledge which is often assumed. It may just be that we need revelation. If this Christian alternative is unthinkable, it merely reflects the mind-set of the thinker.

There is another reason why this larger paradigm is needed. Economists have, for two centuries, been concentrating on the nature of economics, and it is now clear that many of the most important issues in economic life transcend this demarcation. The view which sees the academic disciplines as a lot of tectonic plates rubbing up against one another is just not adequate; economics does not simply sit alongside psychology, sociology and history with an occasional earth-quake at the edges. Economic, social and psychological life are all in reality interwoven in a texture which makes the isolated stance of economic naturalism very unrealistic. More than that, all the deeper issues of life penetrate these specific disciplinary areas so deeply that it is not possible to isolate economic study from a faith commitment. If the philosophy of the Enlightenment has been partly responsible for the fragmentation we now face, an alternative Christian one deserves a hearing.[4]

One of the problems underlying naturalistic economics

was the way it had retreated from value-judgements. A consequence of this position, which claimed to be objective, was to bias the analysis which followed from it, for it excluded from consideration within the discipline all the values on the basis of which people actually made economic decisions. But there was another consequence. For value-free neutral economics meant that there was no ground for self-criticism in the discipline, for whatever is, is good. This stance was actually a working-out of the deeper commitment of the Enlightenment, for if man is the measure of all things, there is no basis upon which human activity can be criticized. This non-critical stance now looks totally insufficient to our task. It is now so evident that things are wrong, and wrong with us, in our economic lives, that value-free complacency is washed away with the tide. The central and pressing question is how we can evaluate ourselves. What basis is there for a self-critical appraisal? But of course the basis lies to hand in the Christian doctrine of sin. God is the measure of man and we can be weighed in the balances and found wanting.

Finally, we note that the crisis in economics, of which the issue of unemployment is a crucial part, is a crisis of values. Despite its declared value-freedom, economics has incorporated many humanist values into its framework — self-interest, progress, maximizing utility, rational decision-making, control and materialism, and there is now enough evidence that these values are in many ways destructive. They are also rapidly changing in a flux of immediate responses to difficult situations. What values should shape the structure of our institutions, the direction of our economic life and the priorities of policy? To ignore the Christian definition of the way we are meant to live, given this situation, is a luxury we can ill afford. In an economic crisis even the prodigal son came to his senses.

One caveat should be entered for all that follows. It is Christian in the sense that it is a response to the truths of biblical revelation, but it is a partial and probably inadequate one. Its main virtue will be that of a blind man who knows he needs a stick. There are many issues which are weakly understood by Christian economists; their lives are compromised by sin and their limitations are many. Yet the need to respond to the problem of the unemployed is so great that at least some attempt must be made. In this spirit we shall therefore consider some of the great themes which shape a Christian approach to economics.

Fatalism or Stewardship?

In the first chapter we considered whether naturalistic economics might be fatalistic in focusing on the mechanical movements of the 'tank'. The deterministic formulation of economic analysis time and time again led to the conclusion that these developments were beyond the control of people. They were onlookers to their economic fate. The Christian alternative to this perspective is quite clear. Rather than being onlookers we are all necessarily participants in economic affairs, and more than that, we are stewards of God's creation and exercise dominion over it. The control is ours. If we have been given responsibility over God's creation, we deny our proper situation if we make ourselves pawns of it. The responsibility to have dominion over the earth, with all the care and obligations which that implies, does not allow us to exonerate ourselves before God from the results of that dominion. The British economy is what we have made; it is constructed from our decisions, by our work, priorities and standards and reflects our attitudes and deepest commitments. To try to move outside this responsibility and become the onlookers, seeking for economic forces which can 'explain' our current predicaments, involves a fundamentally false stance. First, it cuts us off from an awareness of the deepest consequences of our actions. Second, it allows an autonomous power to stand over us to which we surrender our responsibility before God. It gives us over to a God-denying fatalism. This book seeks to affirm that we are totally responsible for the unemployment which surrounds us and we cannot shrug it off as onlookers.

This responsibility, best described by the term 'steward-ship'—our care of God's creation including ourselves—requires a fundamentally different set of attitudes. A dominant attitude today gives priority to self-interest. Look after yourself and things generally will work out fairly well; if they do not, then others can be looked after out of the surpluses generated by the pursuit of personal well-being. It is not surprising that this attitude leads to short-sightedness

70

and that things do not work out as idyllically as the 'invisible hand' model suggests. The Bible invites us to an alternative approach. We are responsible before God for the consequences of our stewardship of God's creation. There are standards of care, respect and neighbourly love to which we are required to submit. We are to love our neighbours as ourselves. These standards are personal and immediate, but are also structural, long-sighted and long-term. They include, for example, the goal 'that there should be no poor in the land'. To open ourselves to this wider concern requires a change of focus. We need to move from an outlook where everything over the garden fence looks blurred, to one where the horizons of our situation are crisply in focus. Once we have made the transition it is obvious how demeaning is the image of self-interested little pawns.[5]

Blessing and Economics

Another major biblical theme which gives a different perspective on economic life is that of dependence on God's blessing. The current dogma is of people who get what they deserve, which carries with it a process of justification, both of self and of economic failure. A Christian perspective begins much further back, with the dependence which we all have on God's blessing, a creation which is rich in food, resources, possibilities and all kinds of daily providence. Basically, all we have is given by God. More proximately we depend on others for our daily blessings. Earlier generations have worked for us, we daily depend on the activities of thousands of other people and we live with technological blessings which are not of our own doing. The issue can be put this way: current economic orthodoxy sees exchange as basic and gift as a peripheral afterthought. Christian economic thinking has to recognize that gift is a far more fundamental category, in terms both of God's blessings to humankind and our human economic organization, which provides the context in which exchange takes place.

This perspective changes the way in which we view economic success. The current view is predominantly materialistic; we achieve economic success by avidly pursuing material satisfaction. We take the direct route. The biblical view of this approach is frankly dismissive. Christ's words were, 'What good is it for a man to gain the whole world and lose his soul?' (Mark 8.36). If you serve Mammon, you get a reward which turns out in the end to be a curse, but if you serve God truly, it is the route to blessing. There are many personal and structural elements to this truth. One of the best-kept sociological secrets today is the torture that exists in the lives and families of the rich. *Dallas* and *Dynasty* glamorize a more sordid reality. We also watch materialist self-interest tearing our institutions apart and fail to question the 'success' of the value. The biblical alternative is: Seek first God's rule and his way of right living and all these things will be given to you as well (Matthew 6.33). On this view the overriding question is, 'How should we live rightly?' not 'How can we make money?' It may be a healthier approach.

Relational Economics
Naturalistic economics has majored on the relationship between persons and goods. It has tended to see economic decisions in terms of individual rational choices between alternatives. Even when it is dealing with institutions like firms, it tends to personify them. They become 'the entrepreneur'. This focus has been accentuated by the dominant economic methods. Maximization techniques, processes of summation, the handling of variables, econometrics and model-building all tend to be incapable of handling relationships between people and institutions. The problem has dominated the history of welfare economics, the dustbin in the discipline into which all the relational problems have been thrown.[6] This bias has grown out of the Enlightenment emphasis on the rational individual, aided by utilitarianism and late-nineteenth-century subjective rationalism. It is clear now that this theoretical fixation is a massive weakness in contemporary theory. Relational questions are treated as 'externalities'. Yet clearly our day-to-day economic lives and decisions do have a profound effect on other people, and it is quite legitimate to take these effects into account when making decisions. We are our brother's and our sister's keeper.

The fundamental biblical interpersonal commandment, 'You shall love your neighbour as yourself' creates the basis for another frame of reference. And it is not an abstract

72

framework, but involves all kinds of detailed interpersonal norms which define how we are rightly to treat one another in economic activity. Some of these, such as the prohibition of stealing, are widely accepted. Others, such as coveting, and the usury laws, are widely ignored. Yet they provide a coherent basis for looking at economic relationships, and especially at the question as to what our attitude is to our neighbour, the unemployed.

Normative Structures

The need is not just for relational economics, but for a new view of economic structures. There is a tendency for the dominance of 'rational' individual decision-making to lead to a preoccupation with summing individual decisions. Both micro- and macro-economic theory has been conceived in these terms. Yet in a mature, interrelated and complex economy this individualistic approach seems incredibly dated. In fact our economic lives are lived to a considerable extent within economic structures, and unless we are free to consider these structures and their direction of development, our economics will be inadequate. Whether it be the family, the nation, the State, the churches, work, taxation, property, markets or firms, they all shape the economy decisively. That families are meant to be institutions of love, nurture and mutual care influences much economic activity. That nations observe norms of neighbourly care and citizenship for their members has profound economic significance. Only by considering the purpose of these institutions explicitly in our analysis will we be able to address the way we actually live.

This raises deep issues. Norms, views about the way we are meant to live, always shape our views of the structures within which we live. What is the purpose of the firm, the bank or national government? Those who actually face the problem will realize that these are the most important economic questions. They signpost where economic institutions are going and the standards which govern their direction. The Bible provides a sweep of revelation about the norms which should shape institutions and structures.[7] This suggests a need to reflect more fundamentally on what our economic structures should be like. It could provide us with an understanding of why things go wrong.

73

As an example, let us briefly consider poverty as a structural problem. Even in the relatively primitive Israelite community at the time of Moses, so that there should be no poor in the land, there were structural prescriptions covering patterns of indebtedness, distribution of land, procedures for employment and self-employment, provision of benefits and controls on accumulation which affected family, nation, state and community. It is clear that far-sightedness meant creating preconditions to prevent and inhibit the growth of poverty and helpless dependence. Stewardship in a biblical sense therefore meant not just loving one's neighbour in immediate personal terms but also through a long-term strategic pattern of care. Abdication of responsibility is ruled out, because it is always our stewardship which shapes our economic system. This and other structural principles act as signposts to our own development.[8] In each of the chapters in Part Two we shall examine the structural principles which do and should operate in various institutional areas.

The Institutional Framework
If we are to do this properly, it is important that we have an overall institutional framework for our analysis. Although, of course, much economic analysis has moved beyond it, there is an amazing tenacity to the economic framework which operates with concepts of the State and individuals. On this view the family is reduced to individual consumers, firms are really entrepreneurs, and the State is the only institution which counts in directing policy. Other agents are acting privately and the State is responsible for overall public policy. A biblical view of normative structures seems to rule out this conception and put the focus on the responsibility of all institutions and all office-holders before God. The result is a plural conception of institutions which cuts across statism on the one hand and the privatized view on the other.[9]

So that we have a firm grasp on this framework it is worth considering the main institutional areas which will be addressed in this next section, which will partly be an exercise in institutional economics. It will soon become evident how important the relationships between these institutions are, and we shall be forced to recognize that many of the relationships in the diagram below are severely neglected in orthodox analysis.

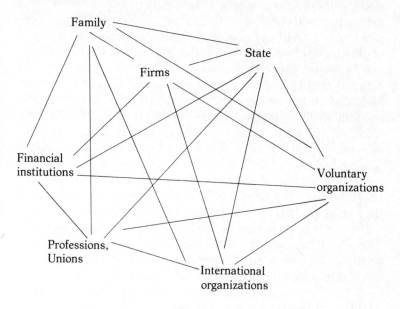

Figure 4

What also needs to be taken into account is how the structure of each of these institutions is unique in a way which shapes the economic activity which they undertake. Further, one of the aims of economic activity is to provide these institutions with the resources they need to fulfil their purposes. Thus the 'economy' is far more embedded in institutional life than is normally acknowledged. This institutional framework is also important because it locates the main areas of discretion in the modern economy. Consequently, it is made the organizing principle for the chapters in this Part Two.

Faith or Sight
Another major change of direction involves the view of time adopted in the discipline. Broadly, in the past it has centred on the concept of rationality. Decision-makers are assumed to gather all the relevant information and make a rational choice

which will lead to the best outcome. Sometimes it is acknowledged that the information is defective, or there is a disagreement about whether 'rational' choice is in terms of means and ends or of a logic of choice. But basically decision-making is a technical process of making the best choice in a slightly erratic world. There is risk and uncertainty, but these can be made predictable. Even the latest formulation — the rational expectations approach — requires people to behave like good value-free economists: a delusion about people and economists.[10] What needs questioning is the basic commitment of economic theory to prediction. It is an unhappy mixture of pride, faith in science, determinism and assumed objectivity which has produced this fixation, but it does not meet the question of what people need from economists. In a limited sense they need predictions, but more fundamentally they need guidance. Where should we be going?

It is time to recognize that we walk by faith, not by sight. The idea that we can sort everything out rationally is a mistake. Our economic future can travel in many different directions and we cannot see round the next corner. We see darkly. When we plan for the future, the outcome is likely to be different from our plans. The very subjects of our economic science also walk by faith — socialism, liberalism, nationalism, conservatism, materialism, transnationalism and many other ideas and values lead people in directions which have greater depth of meaning than the idea of prediction gets close to. What, in retrospect, was the value of the predictions about Britain's entry into the European Community? Thus, on the one hand there is the belief that we can predict and therefore plan, the optimistic arrogance which still dominates the thinking of many economists. On the other hand there is the biblical insistence that we are required to do what is right, seek guidance of God and obey, and the fruits of righteousness will follow.

Economic Sin and Repentance
This, then, is the challenge with which the Christian faith confronts us in our consideration of unemployment. It is not just that our predictions have gone awry, or that the natural equilibrium of the economy has temporarily been knocked off balance. Rather, it is a challenge to the structural development

of the economy and the values and faith which are embodied in it. The biblical word for this misdirection is sin. It is a word which has become so narrowed in its usual secular interpretation that it is worth reconsidering the sheer scope of the term.

Sin is a generic description of the failure of the human response to God, to the creation, to one another and oneself. It involves a breakdown of understanding and attitudes, not just of behaviour. It leads to the decomposition of relationships and institutions. It involves patterns of justification which trap people in false situations because they cannot acknowledge that they are wrong. It leads to false 'idols', which are used to try to create some coherence in disorientated lives. It creates patterns of domination and slavery. It leads to false perceptions. The Bible regularly describes people as being 'lost' in sin. Yet this word is not to be seen as a hammer with which to hit people over the head. It is, rather, a scalpel which cuts to the location of the disease, in our personal lives and more broadly in our communal and structural activity. The biblical doctrine of sin therefore requires us to ask without inhibitions what is wrong in our economy that has caused the blight of unemployment. We may even find that there are false prophets around who are saying 'equilibrium, equilibrium', when there is no equilibrium, and repentance may turn out to be a central economic issue.

The Value of Work

Thus far we have been concerned with general points concerning the paradigm with which economic analysis is approached. Now we focus on the specific subjects with which we are concerned. This brings us to the issue of how we value work. The differences of approach to this question are so striking that they require further consideration. Naturalistic economics treats labour as a commodity which is given a market price within the economic system. A glut of labour, like a glut of tomatoes, needs to be worked through the system. The Marxist reaction to this is to make labour the basis and the measure of all value. The war between these two systems of valuation has dominated world economics for the last century. A Christian response to them focuses on the fact that both make human economic valuation absolute and ultimate. At a gut level we accept this critique every day. We recognize that people are not always paid what they are worth (either too much or too little) in their jobs, and we know that some work produces little of value. In other words, we use more basic criteria of worth to weight the value of work. But this kind of argument needs refining. What work do we value? What is good work?

The characteristic of good work is effective service. As we have moved away from a subsistence economy, we have moved from self-service towards reciprocal service, either directly or through intermediate goods and technology. The positive characteristic of a market economy is that it is an instrument (more or less effective) for extending service, not that it is capitalist or whatever. The service is of one another, and the valuations carried out by a market economy should be to this personal, relational end. We value work directly and indirectly by our service needs, our consumption patterns, investment priorities, research and development and taxes. The indirect nature of job evaluation, where there is no direct product, means that we decide whether many jobs are worthwhile or necessary within a larger institutional or organizational framework. Thus with many paid jobs, as with unpaid ones, we simply decide that they are worth doing. The form of service justifies the good work.[11]

Sometimes the service is not effective, through the attitude of the worker, organizational failure or some larger breakdown. The effectiveness of work can deteriorate long before unemployment appears. What has happened in Britain? It is difficult to know, but there are some signs of deterioration. In the unpaid sector childcare, voluntary work, schoolwork and community work seem to be suffering. In the paid sector we have a high proportion who want to serve, but are not able to. The community suffers a loss of service which must be considerable. (Money-conscious economists would put a figure of £20,000 million each year on it, but the ways of calculating such a figure are many and reflect deeper valuations.) Moreover, the loss of service is regional and hits various groups especially severely, because their valuations, through their poverty, feature much more weakly in market calculations. Others abroad feel less effectively served and are seeking goods elsewhere. Many, probably the majority, feel satisfactorily catered for, with perhaps some complaints over health, education or other forms of service. Some make the point that it is no good creating jobs which are not *real* jobs, and it has to be acknowledged that some, perhaps much, work does not issue in real service. Others make the converse point that there are many real jobs providing urgently needed service, which are just not being done. Certainly, therefore, we are engaged in some kind of failure in service, a deterioration in effective love for our neighbour which the high level of unemployment reflects and illustrates. The deeper task is not just to make more jobs, but more effective service or good work.

Thus far we have considered only the recipients of service. Does work also have a value to those who do it? Classical economics tended to see work as a disutility, a pain which is compensated by pay. Christian values focus on the way work, paid or unpaid, is a normal expression of loving our neighbours as ourselves, that is, a necessary human response. Work also involves the outworking of our responsibilities before God for the creation and for one another. Whether or not work involves toil, and it usually does, it is not an optional part of life, but integral to it. The emphasis in the Mosaic Law was on providing resources to do good work on the assumption that it was necessary. Even though some might live on the illusion that life can be leisure, they soon succeed in turning their leisure into work. Work is not a commodity, but part of us, and its value is centrally bound up with our own value, which also is to be given no commodity status. The provision of good work therefore has its own profound value in our economy.

There is a deeper point. People commit themselves to various kinds of work in acts of faith. The education, training and experience required for most jobs takes a decade and a half, and for some jobs twice that period. People have faith in, give themselves to, and invest in their jobs. The terms 'vocation' and 'calling' actually describe what people feel, or would like to feel, about their daily task. The meaning of the way they spend nearly half their waking life is crucial to their relationship with God, themselves and their neighbours. Personal commitment like this cannot be treated in a cavalier fashion, for we are talking of the value of people and not disposable goods and chattels. If good work is to be valued in this way, the question remains as to whether actual market valuations approximate these priorities or not.

Unemployment—the Parable of the Workers in the Vineyard

Finally, let us come directly to the concern of this book. The issue of unemployment was directly addressed by Christ in the parable of the workers in the vineyard. As Jesus explained to the crowd, the rule of God is like a landowner who went out to employ men to work. He employed some, but later when he went out there were others idle, and so he employed them, promising to pay them their due. Three times later in the day he went out and found others who had no one to employ them, and on each occasion he set them to work. At the end of the day, when they came for their wages, he gave them each the same pay. Those who had worked the whole day expected to receive more than the others, but the landowner was firm in saying that they had not been treated unfairly. He had the right to give to the last worker the same as to the earlier ones. They should not be envious, because the employer had been generous. So, concluded Christ, the last will be first and the first will be last.

Some will say that this parable was not concerned with the issue of employment, and in a deeper sense this is not its focus. The example taken in the parable is of far wider significance. The landowner is a picture of God, and the message which comes across indelibly is that narrow human conceptions of deserving fall down in the face of God's generous dealings with his creatures. The priority, we learn, is with those who are last. The difference between God's concern with us and our narrow conceptions of deserving is striking, and is reflected in every area of life. To narrow this parable to a literal concern with employment would be a travesty of the teaching. Yet, simply because of the scope of this teaching, it is entirely in order to apply it also to the issue of employment, as the parable shows. The priority, God says, is not those who have built up their own ideas of what they deserve as a result of their work, but those who have no one to employ them. Our response should reflect God's attitude.

If we pause at this point, the challenge is obvious. Are the first to be first or are the first to be last? With the imperative of this teaching before us, let us begin to look in institutional terms at what is happening in our economy and suggest why unemployment is so high.

Notes

1. M. Blaug, *The Methodology of Economics* (Cambridge University Press 1980), p. 253.
2. See F. Suppe, *The Structure of Scientific Theories* (University of Illinois Press 1977), pp. 3—241; B. Caldwell, *Beyond Positivism* (George Allen and Unwin 1982). This theme is more adequately treated in my Ph.D thesis 'Foundational Epistemologies in Consumption Theory' (Free University, Amsterdam).
3. N. Wolterstorff, *Reason within the Bounds of Religion* (Eerdmans 1976) states the argument nicely.
4. See H. Dooyeweerd, *A New Critique of Theoretical Thought*, vols. 1—3 (Pres. and Reformed 1953) for the definitive treatment of this issue.
5. For the development of the meaning of stewardship see B. Goudzwaard, *Capitalism and Progress* (Eerdmans 1981).
6. See E. J. Mishan, 'A Survey of Welfare Economics, 1939—59', in *Surveys of Economic Theory*, vol. i (Macmillan 1965), pp. 154—222; A. Sen, 'Interpersonal Comparisons of Welfare' in M. J. Boskin (ed.), *Economics and Human Welfare* (Academic Press 1979), pp. 183—201; A. Storkey, 'The Neighbour Welfare Criterion' (Economics Faculty, Calvin).
7. See A. Storkey, *Christian Social Perspective*, pp. 122—50, 290—319, 335—78; C. Wright, *Living as the People of God* (IVP 1983); and M. Schluter, *Jubilee Papers* (Jubilee Centre, Cambridge).
8. See B. Goudzwaard, *Aid for the Overdeveloped West* (Wedge 1975); R. Mullin, *The Wealth of Christians* (Paternoster 1983) for a pre-economic consideration; R. Sider, *Rich Christians in an Age of Hunger* (IVP 1979) for a pre-structural one; J. Stott, *Issues facing Christians Today* (Marshalls 1984), pp. 122—38, 154—94, 212—33; and B. Griffiths, *The Creation of Wealth* (Hodder and Stoughton 1984).
9. J. Skillen, 'Politics, Pluralism and the Ordinances of God' in H. van der Goot (ed.), *Life is Religion* (Paideia Press 1981); A. Storkey, ibid., pp. 140—3.
10. Or proves that people are slaves to defunct economists.
11. See P. Marshall *et al.*, *Labour of Love* (Wedge 1980); F. Schumacher, *Good Work* (Abacus 1980); J. Stott, ibid., pp.

154—72; R. H. Tawney, *The Acquisitive Society* (G. Bell 1921); and J. Ruskin, *Unto This Last*, 1862 (George Allen 1900), pp. 1—37 for some fuller statements of this theme.

6:   Financial Empires

What are Banks and Financial Institutions For?
This seems an elementary and even silly question to ask. Of course we know: they have been about for centuries and the answer is obvious. But is it? Let us look at the official mechanistic answer. Banks are profit-making firms which are involved in the use, borrowing and lending of money. They borrow and lend money and make profits from their transactions. This may seem straightforward, but it is not so. Firms normally supply goods, but banks supply and demand money; they are institutions which operate on both sides of the market. Firms merely sell goods, but banks, in lending, are involved in making judgements and using discretion about those to whom they make advances. You might even say they have faith in their clients. Moreover, since it is usually other people's money they are lending, there is a unique set of obligations and responsibilities which they exercise in the use of funds towards the wider community. When we recognize these points, the myopic, profit-maximizing view of banking becomes somewhat limited.

Nor is it the only false image. We have been taught that the market for money is one of the most perfect and competitive markets there is. In a limited sense this is half-true, but we need the fuller truth. First, the market is heavily influenced by the government. Second, banks and other financial institutions are also often big enough to influence the structure of the markets in which they operate. Third, as institutions they have the resources and the scope to exercise considerable discretion in their market policies.[1] Thus, rather than being mere pawns in a vast system of economic forces, banks and other financial institutions shape what goes on in decisive and important ways. If this is the case, we need to ask what are the values and priorities of banks? What are the ethos and guiding principles by which banks operate? We can be sure it will affect monetary policy, investment patterns and also employment. 'What are banks for?' remains an important and central question.

Before we go further, it is worth taking some biblical

bearings on the issue. Let us briefly consider the significance of the biblical usury laws. There is debate which goes back beyond Calvin about the question of whether interest should be charged on loans.[2] For our present purposes we can ignore that aspect of the issue. The key point about these laws was the purpose of lending. The emphasis of the Mosaic Law was on the wide distribution of resources so that everyone should have a means of livelihood. The overall guiding norm was the following:

However, there should be no poor among you, for in the land the Lord your God is giving you to possess as your inheritance, he will richly bless you, if only you fully obey the Lord your God and are careful to follow all these commands I am giving you today. (Deut. 15.4−5)

Specifically it meant:

If there is a poor man among your brothers in any of the towns of the land that the Lord your God is giving you, do not be hardhearted or tightfisted towards your poor brother. Rather be openhanded and freely lend him whatever he needs. (Deut. 15.7−8)

There was to be no interest and no pressure to repay. In addition there was a prescription which will cause consternation among bankers, namely, the requirement that debts which cannot be repaid be cancelled every seven years. (It is ironic that this—an unthinkable thought for bankers—will actually have to happen in some debtor nations.) There is, however, no need to focus on the details of this law, except to note that they were given into a context where surplus funds were diamond scarce in relation to our own. The point is that the normative purpose of lending was to help those in need to meet their necessities and earn their livelihood. There were and are other more sophisticated reasons for lending, but this communal concern was a normal part of the Mosaic banking system. 'Banking' was not profit directed, but a part of a process of making available to those who needed them the resources for earning a livelihood. Nor was this so short-sighted, for the strength of banking depends on the overall strength of the economy. Neighbourly care may be more long-sighted than profit-maximization.

84

Has this kind of concern been a dominant part of the ethos of British banking?

Banks and Financial Institutions

The answer is, of course, no. Everybody knows that the banks do not have helping the needy as their priority. Their concern tends to be with themselves as institutions and their own profitability. Many of them now constitute massive empires with self-referring goals. The extent to which this might be a problem is rarely faced, because the naturalistic model assumes that maximizing profit leads to the best of all possible worlds, including fuller employment. There is, however, a much simpler interpretation of the situation; when banks ignore the responsibility to help those who need resources, in time the base of viable economic enterprise shrinks, and the possibilities of lending become even smaller, unless they are undertaken abroad. It may even be that banks and financial institutions actually hinder the growth of enterprise and employment. How might this be?

(a) The Internal Transfers of Banks

Normal Keynesian macroeconomic analysis looks at exchange or public transfers of income and expenditure. Nevertheless, in the modern economy transfers within some institutions are as important as these public flows and have a substantial impact on income and expenditure. If we consider the flows within banks and other financial institutions, it is not difficult to see how significant they are. Within their own accounts the financial institutions move funds on a scale which is of major strategic importance. One of the effects is geographical. Generally speaking, we can expect funds deposited with banks or building societies in one part of the country to be redistributed in a way which leads to substantial geographical relocation of those funds. We can guess what the effect will be. But the word is 'guess', for the banks keep this kind of information a secret between themselves and their computers. Funds put into the banks, building societies and pension funds in areas of high unemployment will move away to areas of high profitability in the south, the City or overseas. The scale of this movement must be considerable. Hundreds

85

of millions of pounds loaned on low or zero interest rates are moved out of depressed areas to the south-east, New York or wherever. If this is happening on any scale, areas of the country must be permanently leeched of their economic lifeblood.

The failure to take this movement seriously is somewhat puzzling. In the United States 'green-lining' legislation has required both information and firm control of movements of funds. Yet the banking system in the United States involves many more and far more local banks, which would transmit funds much less easily across the nation. Despite the more *laissez-faire* approach to government, the United States has long faced this issue. The British pattern of centralized, near-monopolistic banking, however, goes unmonitored. This can only be because the myth of neutral banking continues to dull our consciousness.

What does this mean on the ground in Britain? In the north-east, Liverpool and Glasgow the funds generated by the communities are clinically eliminated from the area, cutting out sources of investment, expenditure and personal capital. Building societies' policies have been geared against lending on older property in areas where prices are less buoyant. Banks look askance at investment in these areas — meanwhile money gravitates to expensive property areas, pushing up prices further in a self-fulfilling prophecy of sound policy while temples to banking soar in the City or the New World. Clearly, there is an issue of justice here. Citizens pay funds into the banks which whisk them out of the area and eliminate what is desperately needed to build up the local economy. Of course, one can say 'Let the buyer of these services beware' and leave the onus with the banking public, but with such a massive banking monopoly, there is little discretion for the customer. The ethos of the banks is not merely one of not caring about the needs of depressed areas, it is probably one which is actively destructive of their ability to recover and grow. In effect, the poor are lending to the rich at near zero rates of interest.

(b) Centralized Decision-Making
But there is more to the pattern than this. The Big Four banks and other financial institutions have developed a new

organizational pattern. Increasingly the lending decisions are made centrally. The central financial analysts handle a high proportion of investment decisions and local bank managers become the pawns handling the small change and the local customers who are worth dealing with. There are plausible profit-making reasons for this development. Why employ a lot of local bank managers to make thousands of small decisions when the same kind of return can be made on one decision to hold funds in another currency? The more centralized decision-making process seems a more efficient and a better one.

Financial analysis also has an ethos and direction of its own. Its aim is a process of calculating a guaranteed rate of return which is higher than normal. There is an array of techniques for minimizing or eliminating risk. They are predictive models which are statistical, based on market behaviour, or focus on key financial variables, which work tolerably well. But rarely do these models get behind the financial veil to the economic reality to which they are related. Often group psychology is far more important than the productive performance of companies in deciding the success of a portfolio selection. Thus the framework of analysis and the tools of expertise developed in the central decision-making units of banks lead away from direct job-creating investment decisions into financial management. When we consider the likely impact of this organizational pattern on jobs, the picture is not encouraging. Job-creating investment in many cases is small-scale and local. Yet it is precisely this kind of investment which the banks and other institutions have a reduced ability to handle and probably much less interest in considering. Conversely, handling funds in the City, the European Market, Tokyo or New York is attractive and fits the skills of the whiz-kids with calculators who keep the financial markets of the world churning sleeplessly. The idea that these persons should be concerned about local industry and employment is absurd, a fleeting thought which slides across suburban train windows on the way home. Thus, by its organizational concentration and the ethos of the financial analysts, investment which would promote job creation cannot and does not happen.

(c) The Direction of Lending

The strategic direction of bank lending has also had a decisive effect. The trends have been towards property, overseas investment, private consumers and trading wealth. Let us examine these. Bank lending patterns show a very conservative orientation. One of the premises is that lending should be secured, wherever possible, by the government or some other safe institution usually backed by property, thus automatically favouring those who are established against those who are not. This reinforces the division between financial and industrial capitalism. Compared with their European and Japanese counterparts British bankers have an aversion to lending long to industry. This is probably partly because in their training they have not been prepared to come to terms with the details of industrial enterprise; they are not secure with more than company accounts. Property and security dominate real industrial considerations.

There is also a bias overseas. Partly, central investment specialists are more willing to take risks in South America or the Far East, where bad debts can be written off as part of a wide portfolio, than local managers are in Oldham or Doncaster. But falling and fluctuating exchange rates have also made potential returns overseas greater than domestic returns, in the short run at least. Possibly financial institutions are fitting in with Britain's post-industrial label; if Britain is a poor market and industrial base, then why not go elsewhere?

At the same time there has been a strong trend towards advances to private customers for consumption-orientated borrowing. There have been pressures towards this from inflation, rising incomes, leisure and luxury family living, but there is also no doubt about the efforts the banks have put into opening up customer credit. As a result the well-secured individual wanting finance for a yacht tends to get priority over an expanding but wobbly local partnership. This emphasis on consumption-related lending, much of which has then been spent overseas, has had a long-term effect on the possibilities for investment. This trend will be difficult to reverse, for organizational reasons.

It is possible that the banks are also conservative in the sense that they distrust labour. The kinds of advances or investments which are congenial are those which do not depend on or use labour overmuch. Labour is unreliable, unpredictable and can demand its own cut of success. Property is far better; the concern there is with a straight return on an asset. One could guess that there is a subtle but substantial bias in the banks' pattern of lending away from the kinds of labour that bankers do not like politically and towards those which are more congenial, or to pleasant, quiescent bits of property. The blighted areas of the north may well in part be explained by the biases of conservative middle-class banking.

The Banks and Inflation

One of the most neglected concepts in economics is the idea of 'seigniorage'. It denotes the fact that when money is created, the institution which first brings it into use gets a windfall profit of the value of the money. Simply by printing it they have command over goods and services to the face value of the notes that are printed. The way in which governments in the 1960s and 1970s used this process as a way of financing increased expenditure has, of course, been one of the main focuses of the monetarist critique. Yet alongside this critique of the government has been a silence about the seigniorage effects on the banks themselves for, as every young economist knows, most of the money in the economy is not Bank of England notes and coin but credit operating within the banking system. And, as they also know, there is a credit multiplier operating on the cash base which means that the banks can create several times as much credit as the cash base. Since 1970 there have also been reforms which have increased the ratio of credit to cash. Now this has not in any sense been the fault of the banks and financial institutions, but the result is one which needs to be recognized. The outcome has been that a seigniorage effect has accrued to the banks on a scale that far surpasses that which accrued to the government. They have had a massive windfall as a result of the process of money creation.[3]

The actual effects of this process were very complex. They led, in part, to the rapid expansion of banks and financial institutions and their high level of profits during that period. Indeed, this seigniorage process has helped create a financial

89

sector. It meant that lending and borrowing became temporarily more profitable and as a result certain forms of assets experienced massive capital gains. This process has generated other trends, none of which seems particularly healthy. The first is the disjunction between finance and long-term investment. Changes in interest rates, exchange rates, rates of inflation and capital values mean that the return on funds is more likely to be decided by these price fluctuations than by the long-term outcome of the actual use of funds. There comes a time when the dissociation of finance and investment becomes serious; it has probably already arrived. The banking ethos of speculative financial management encourages this unstable pattern. Unexpected events could make it more serious. As the ratio of hot money to solid finance climbs on the world's money markets, the question arises as to whether banks really know how fragile is the base on which much of their lending rests.

At the same time this point gives the lie to monetarism. The financial institutions do have coinsiderable discretion, and attempts at mechanical control by the central bank are bound to be limited. In a situation where most of the money in the system is created by the banks, who have international resources anyway, the kind of mechanical control envisaged by monetarists is just not realistic. In fact the early 1980s show that governments with a monetarist commitment have only flabby control of credit, especially because of the seigniorage effect, which they have not acted to control. This raises the question of the internal control of these institutions. They cannot just be turned on and off like taps, but need an internal structure which allows them to act responsibly. At present they are responsible to their shareholders and no one else. Is there a broader pattern of accountability which should be built in the structure of banks and financial institutions?

Finally, there is a big question beside the dominant ethos in British banking. It is often a narrow, City-based approach which ignores and misconceives many of the principles involved in financial markets. The influence of its ethos through monetarist policy has in many ways been destructive, and it may be that the practice of banking is already caught in its own illusions and adding to unemployment.

The Stock Exchange
Jobs depend crucially upon the capital base of companies and their investment programmes. Much of this comes from reinvested profits, but a great deal depends on the institution which is formally at the centre of the process of raising capital, the Stock Exchange. How effective are the Stock Exchange and related institutions in generating the kind of investment which is needed to expand and effectively use the workforce? Again, we find institutional pressures which may be having the opposite effect.

(a) Pressures of Scale
The first thing that has to be noticed is that the Stock Exchange deals only in large 'quoted' companies. Through élitism, high charges and probably self-importance it does not touch the level of business which, since the time of the Macmillan Committee, has been closely associated with job creation. The Wilson Committee pointed out the same failing. One of the reasons for this emphasis is the buying pattern of the big institutions, the pension funds, insurance companies and unit trusts. They tend to go for the blue chip companies and consolidate a large conservative bias. It is not just economies of scale but the orientation to shareholding. With respect to the question of employment the Stock Exchange does not really touch the potentially dynamic area.

(b) The Structure of Share Capital
There is, however, a more fundamental problem than this. It relates to the actual definition of what is traded on the Stock Exchange. In a normal company the capital invested in the enterprise may last twenty, ten or even five years, and most companies write off investment over relatively short periods (partly because of tax incentives). The evaluation of investment is a relatively dynamic process. By contrast, shares last for ever. As a result the Stock Exchange is actually dealing in dead stock, which no longer represents the actual investment going on now, but the overall historic situation of the company. As time passes and economies become more mature, the structure of the Stock Exchange is increasingly tied to the capital value of these historical assets and does not allow the current investment needs of a company to be

reflected in the market. The Stock Exchange is trading shares on the basis of their current overall performance, rather than the viability of future investments.[4] This works satisfactorily when the market is buoyant overall, but during periods of depression the market is actually very poor at responding to future investment needs. New issues can only take place successfully on the basis of obvious company success and a buoyant position in the market generally. Thus regularly there are years of dearth of new issues, and one is due at the end of the 1980s. During this time the contribution to industrial investment through the share market will be negligible.

One way out of this problem is to have a relatively high proportion of shares which are amortized at the end of a certain lifetime. This, of course, changes the emphasis in the stock market from gains in capital value to flow of income over the lifetime of the share. (It is interesting that fixed-life bonds play a far larger role in the capital markets of quite a few European countries.)[5] This would move the bias away from trading on the historical pattern of ownership towards meeting current investment needs. Meanwhile we face the fact that, if this analysis is correct, the actual structure of Stock Exchange dealings militates against an efficient and forward-looking deployment of capital.

(c) Fluctuations in Share Values

However, this is not the end of the story. The emphasis in the market is on capital values, and periodically these rise and fall. We note that the fluctuations in market share values are often massively greater than the fluctuations in the value of the underlying assets of most major companies.[6] This is partly because of the structure of share capital which we have just examined and also because of the distribution of risk-carrying in companies. What happens when these fluctuations in paper values take place? In terms of real flows the pattern is very complicated. In one sense for everybody who sells, at whatever price, somebody also buys, and so there is no 'effect' on income flows. Yet there *is* an effect. When a large rise in share prices takes place there is a heavy redistribution of wealth (and partly of income) towards a minority group in the population. What do they do with it?

Some, of course, try to buy into what they hope will be larger capital gains. Others diversify into different assets or realize them in personal wealth. Because shares can be instantly disposed of there is a recognition that the market is inherently unstable and can soon change. The effects of this process are difficult to gauge, but they are something like the following. During periods of booming share prices wealth is redistributed to a group of people who have no direct relation with and little interest or concern with job-related investment. It is also sucked into this swollen heap of dead shares in a way which leaves relatively little available for genuinely new investment. During periods of low share prices the possibility of investment is effectively frozen. Although the market is finely tuned to the task of profiteering, in terms of its ability to stimulate and allocate investment for jobs it is an ass.

Were it not that the pension funds and other major institutional stock holders impose some kind of stability on the market, its inadequate framework would be glaringly obvious. When it next enters into serious decline, its weaknesses will be unavoidable.

(d) Company Control

A final problematic area is company control. There is a whole range of situations where takeovers occur or are threatened because of the market weakness of the particular company, rather than through any inherent weakness. Indeed, a successful company may well find itself threatened, especially if it does not conform to market behaviour by realizing dividends and continually ploughs back profits. Other companies whose market value happens to be low are gobbled up and find assets sold off in order to realize quick profits. Especially with a large number of companies owned abroad, it becomes evident that this pattern of control often makes little economic sense to the companies who are its pawns and the workers who contribute to them.

What again emerges is the way in which this institution, reverentially uncritical of itself, is fundamentally failing in its ability to provide investable funds for British business and industry. Its increasingly short-sighted preoccupation with maximizing financial profit has something of the character of fiddling while the violin's on fire. The idea of the longer term needs and development of industry gets lost in the immediate fluctuations of the market. This situation has been compounded in the late 1980s by the fact that much of the City's funds have been soaked up by the flotation of denationalized companies. None of this money gets remotely near to being actual new investment.

Conclusion

We have seen something of the importance of these financial institutions, and of their discretion for holding and directing funds. Indeed, we have seen how the Stock Exchange can absorb massive amounts of saving which do not issue in investment and how the banks can redirect savings into consumer credit. This discretion is not something which the government can control in a mechanical way, nor does it only operate in one dimension. It involves the use of a wide range of resources under the guidance of principles of banking and investment.

Closer examination of the ethos of these institutions has shown that they are inadequate to address the needs of the unemployed. Indeed, they seem actively to work against the cause of those who need work. While the temples to money soar in the City, factories are flattened in the provinces. The value of money is adulated and the value of work ignored. We can observe the effects of structural sin in these institutions, but we can also go a step further and work for their reform. As the illusions of financial neutrality become more obvious, this sober task will become more compelling.

Notes

1. This is making the point in institutional terms. The normal terms of the discussion are the inadequacies of the IS-LM frame of analysis. A discretionary market model goes beyond Hicks's fixprice and other qualifications—see John Hicks, 'IS-LM: An Explanation', *Journal of Post-Keynesian Economics*, vol. iii, Winter 1980 — 1.
2. See F. Graham, *The Constructive Revolutionary* (John Knox Press 1971).
3. This suggests that monetarism might be more a reaction to the changes of competition and credit control in the early 1970s and

to the seigniorage effect than to fiscal expansionism. It is shooting at the wrong target. See Chapter 12.

4. This is a development of G. Goyder's thinking. See *The Future of Private Enterprise* (OUP 1951) and *The Responsible Company* (OUP 1961).

5. See IBRO, *Banking Systems Abroad* (1978), pp. 69–70, 181, 212.

6. For a defence of the capital market from a City viewpoint see R. Brealey, 'The Efficiency of the British Capital Market', in *City Lights* (IEA 1979), pp. 21–37.

7: Profit and Loss

The Conventional View of the Firm

On the oldest conventional model the firm aims at the maximization of profit. This, according to classical and neo-classical theory is the dominant, normal and natural aim of all firms, which are assumed to be run by a single capitalist-entrepreneur. Since the 1930s it has become more sophisticated, taking account of growth, patterns of managerial control and various organizational goals, but basically it has stayed within the profit-maximizing form. Another crucial part of this model is that labour should be treated, along with capital and raw materials, as a factor of production to be manipulated to achieve optimum levels of output. Workers provide the input of labour, which can be treated in a detached, objective and impersonal way. Although contemporary approaches are less strident, the same ideology holds sway in business courses throughout the land. The assumed goal is profit-maximization, workers are treated as a variable factor of production and decision-making is through centralized entrepreneurial control. Indeed, there seems to be a growth of adulation of the centralized decision-maker. Consequently, finance and accounting are the basis on which real decisions are made, and external costs and benefits are ignored in a basically private profit-making frame of reference. Often personnel management is given the task of putting a human face to an essentially inhuman view of the firm.

Although this is the dominant ideology, is it actually the correct understanding of a company? Again, many business-men would regard it as preposterous even to ask the question — to challenge profit-maximization is to propound the normal soft leftist nonsense. But challenge it we must. Again we ask, what is a company for? When we do this, it is possible to see a major category mistake in the contemporary business and economic conception. The company must be for others; it cannot be for itself. The naturalistic model says that a company seeks its own self-interest, serves itself and makes a profit, but coincidentally finishes up being of benefit to others. But this is a peculiar inversion of what must go on. It is like

97

saying that the violinist played the violin in order to bow properly. The larger and prior conception must be the service which the company provides for others, within which the profits or blessings of the company have meaning. Now this is no slick distinction, although many will feel that of course profits and service are both part of business. The question at issue is the conception, attitudes, motives and approach to business, and the capitalist view which dominates much British and American thinking is fundamentally defective as a frame of reference.

First, the autocentric reference point makes the orientation unresponsive. Instead of its motivation being towards service, the needs of others and the best way to meet those needs, the company is contemplating its own profit-making navel. Second, it tends to be short-sighted. The focus is on immediate profit, but the oft-repeated lesson of business is that profits follow, often a long way behind, commitment to meeting a particular need, product development or research and development. The profit fixation can often be a hindrance to sound long-term decisions. Further, the profit motive actually changes market activity in a destructive direction. Companies engineer monopolies, try to corner markets, develop restrictive market practices, oversell goods and reduce their quality. It has a tendency to disregard effects which are harmful to others. The attitude has long been noted. Engels described it thus in the mid nineteenth century:

I have never seen a class so deeply demoralized, so incurably based on selfishness, so corroded within, so incapable of progress, as the English bourgeoisie; and I mean by this the bourgeoisie proper, particularly the Liberal, Corn Law-repealing bourgeoisie. For it nothing exists in this world, except for the sake of money, itself not excluded. It knows no bliss save that of rapid gain, no pain save that of losing gold. In the presence of this avarice and lust of gain, it is not possible for a single human sentiment or opinion to remain untainted. True, these English bourgeois are good husbands and family men, and have all sorts of other private virtues, and appear, in ordinary discourse, as decent and respectable as all other bourgeois; even in business they are better to deal with than the Germans; they do not higgle and haggle so much as our own pettifogging merchants; but how does this help matters? Ultimately it is self-interest, and especially money gain, which alone determines them. I once went to Manchester with such a bourgeois, and spoke to him of the bad, unwholesome method of building, the frightful condition of the working-people's quarters, and asserted that I had never seen so ill-built a city. The man listened quietly to the end, and said at the corner when we parted: 'And yet there is a great deal of money made here; good morning, sir.'[1]

The point is not just that this attitude is widespread, but also that it is the official orthodoxy. This is how business says it lives. Yet this position is false at two levels. First, those who have been committed to it in Britain have seen other nations which make service the priority pass them by in industrial development. Precisely at the point of service British industry is repeatedly criticized and found wanting. In this sense the model has failed us. But in another sense it remains inaccurate, because this is not how companies behave. Necessarily they make a range of judgements about how they should and can best serve the wider community, largely in terms of the goods and services they supply, but also in other ways, like the provision of work. It is time that this deeper conception of what the business enterprise is meant to be is fully stated.

The Normative Purpose of the Company

The orthodox interpretation of post-industrial economic history is so deeply ingrained in all of us that it seems outrageous to challenge it. That history, we are told, is capitalist and the success of the modern West is the success of capitalism. The only alternative, it seems, is socialist or Marxist, which by most standards has been far less successful. Yet, it is possible that this history is basically flawed. It may be that the success of the modern West, whatever that means, is the success of the ethic of service, not primarily of capitalism. Let us trace something of that history.

It has its origin in the great New Testament theme of being servants one of another. Listen to Paul's teaching on the theme: although it is specifically applied to the Church, it has universal sigificance for those who will listen.

There are different kinds of gifts, but the same Spirit. There are different kinds of service, but the same Lord. There are different kinds of working, but the same God works all of them in all men . . . Now the body is not made up of one part, but of many. If the foot should say, 'Because I am not a hand, I do not belong to the body,' it would not for that reason cease to be part of the body. And if the ear should say, 'Because I am not an eye, I do not belong to the body,' it would not for that reason cease to be part of the body. If the whole body were an eye, where would the sense of hearing be? If the whole body were an ear, where would the sense of smell be? But in fact God has arranged the parts of the body, every one of them, just as he wanted them to be . . . But God has combined the members of the body and has given greater honour to the parts that lacked it, so that there should be no division in the body, but that its parts should have equal concern for one another. (1 Cor. 12.4−25)

Service and love and trust, we learn, issue in a variety of gifts, a pattern of division of labour, mutual help and trust. It may be that Max Weber in his famous interpretation of the relationship between Protestantism and modern economic development missed the underlying transition.[2] In the period after the Reformation it seems that there was enough growth in diversified service and mutual trust for economies to translate from a largely subsistence basis into one of extended mutual service. The process was so diffuse and difficult to identify that it is not surprising that it was unnoticed. The crucial transition to the modern economy was the opening-up of a division of service, rather than crude entrepreneurial spirit. As Weber and others noted, the Puritan doctrine of 'calling', serving God and one's fellows with all one's heart, was part of the development of economic enterprise, but this too was often in a context of responsible service rather than self-seeking aggrandizement. Could it be that we have been so beguiled by Adam Smith's Enlightenment doctrine of self-interest as preached by generations of self-justifying entre-preneurs, that we have ignored the role of the humble biblical norm 'you shall love your neighbour as yourself' in generating the industrial explosion of the West in the last two centuries?

If this is the case, the ideology of capitalism becomes a form of special pleading. It is not entrepreneurial decision-making, risk-taking or the accumulation of capital but the extension, albeit defectively, of the biblical principle of loving one's neighbour and mutual service which is behind the 'success' of the West economically. Rather than the capitalists being able to look around them and say 'This is our handiwork', the reality is that the ethic of service, among workers, managers and the rest has produced its long-term historical fruit.[3] Of course, in more recent years this ethic has been compromised by the priority given to self-service, and other countries have understood better than Britain what the ethic involves. But when we move from an ideological framework which centres on profit-making capitalism to one which centres on service, a lot of things become clearer, including our understanding of what a company is.

We recognize that the guiding norm of the company is service, not profit. Companies succeed because they serve their customers and that is their *raison d'être*. A company is a community of people which serves the wider public through the provision of goods or services. Failure to do so, or to do it as well as others, means in one sense or another failure of the company. Conversely, the developing of new forms of service is the dynamic of company growth. Second, a company is internally a service unit. Workers, shareholders, the wider community, managers and also consumers relate together in a framework of trust, respect and organic contribution. Sometimes the trust and mutuality may break down, in a strike or whatever, but that merely shows how centrally significant this element is. One of the discoveries over the last decade is the way in which these norms are more successfully established in the company practice of our most successful national competitors like Japan and Germany. Even this very cursory analysis confirms that companies can only be realistically seen as communities with a plurality of distinct but related service aims.

If this is the case, this reality should be built into our basic Christian model of the company.[4] They can be seen as having a variety of aims clustering round the central norm of service, including perhaps the following:

The scope of service provided (measured perhaps by sales)
The quality of goods or service
Growth in the resource base of the company

Thrift and efficiency in the use of resources
The provision of meaningful work
A secure future for the company
A well-rewarded and well-treated workforce
Fair treatment of those who contribute resources
Responsible development of capital and technology
Service to the wider community
Increased employment.

A company might not subscribe to all of these aims or it may have others, but essentially it must respond to the central norm of service and consequently establish priorities among these various aims. Immediately we can see how these aims are dynamically related and lead to each company having a distinct profile. For example, one company might see thrift and efficiency reflected in low prices as its major contribution to the wider community. Another might focus on the development of capital and technology as a way of establishing a secure future for the company. What is clear is the way that as a company succeeds in various areas, its discretionary power grows. Conversely, failure in some of these aims can leave a company with much less scope for exercising its discretion. Nevertheless, it will still have a strategy for development, which may design new goals in some areas and more limited activity in others. The following diagram will give an approximation of what is going on.

Many economists and businessmen would readily subscribe to this kind of model as a more realistic description of the way in which a company develops and decisions are weighed. Real business has this kind of complexity. But what this model undermines once and for all is the determinist capitalist ideology that employment is not a company goal or that the route to fuller employment has to be that of making companies profitable so that they grow and can employ more workers — the be-good-and-do-what-you-are-told syndrome. If a company decides to contract employment, that is its choice; it is not merely a reaction to economic forces. There is a range of strategies which companies can adopt to address the problem of unemployment, and they do not automatically involve toeing the line of the shareholders. Primarily, they need to be strategies for a growth in service.

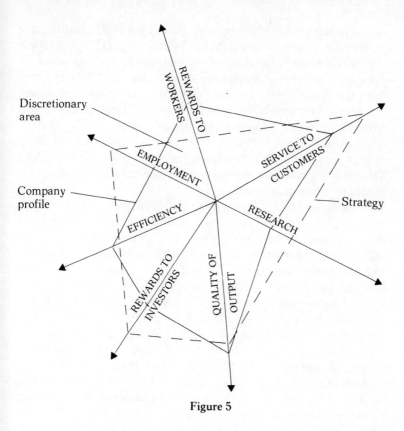

Figure 5

Company Service

Everybody knows what is wrong with British industry. The workforce has a low commitment to the aims of the company and, as soon as surplus funds are available, makes sure that they can be pushed into the wage packet. They resist attempts to work more efficiently and to economize on labour. Conversely the directors often have a weak long-term strategy and fail to mobilize the workforce properly. Although there are companies where everything works well and co-operation is effective, an ideological divide passing right down the middle of the company is normal, and it has cost billions in lost production and suboptimal performance. In this adversarial world the first thing to suffer is the customer; the self-interest of the contending parties means that the consumer takes a back seat in terms of price, service, quality and market awareness. So the divided goals of profit-maximizing and worker rewards have left service of the consumer a low priority. Everybody knows what is wrong, but at the same time the ideology to which bankers, capitalists and many Conservatives subscribe *must* lead to this conclusion. This is why much of the rhetoric which is directed at 'turning Britain around' is so empty. It is generated from an egocentric base of self-service, which produces the response — why bother? Thus the norm which should provide the central meaning of a company often gets lost.

Some companies have been successful by imposing a system of power relationships and muted threats which keep most people in line, and others make sure that there are enough employees sweetened with pay and benefits sufficient to keep them happy. But the pattern does not really work. Underlying it, as everybody knows, is a pattern of self-interest for the shareholders, the managers and the workforce. This self-interest works its way through in relation to the consumers in the form of poor-quality work, substandard research and development, poor aftersales service and other forms of casual attitude to the customer. In time the underlying attitude becomes evident. The self-interest which is the cornerstone of neo-classical and Conservative economic thinking creates a short-sighted and destructive pattern of events with a nominal and inadequate commitment of the workers to the customers. Thus the very attitude which is lauded in *laissez-faire* Conservative economics turns out to produce futile competition between management and workforce in the firm. The values present in British company ideology have merely produced their rotten fruit. The biblical norm, You shall love your neighbour as yourself, has been slighted.

This failure of service is partly one of attitude, growing out of the complacency of an established, self-reverential business class, but it is also a structural problem. For the crucial questions, especially in relation to unemployment, are, Who should be served, and how can they best be served? Here are the real dynamic questions, but they remain on the periphery of vision of the average company.

Service and Employment

The problem now begins to emerge with greater clarity. Partly because of the priority given to profits and partly because of the bitter experience of the adversarial situation in much of British industry, there has been a quite systematic policy of labour elimination in many companies. If they can reduce dependence on the workforce, then the whole operation becomes more viable. If ten workers paid at £6,000 per annum are replaced by five paid at £12,000 per annum, the latter will be tied by their affluence to greater company loyalty. It is in the self-interest of the company to eliminate workers in this way, even if the technological costs are high, and the result is more unemployed. This tendency has been encouraged by the generous terms on which firms have been allowed to write off capital expenditure for tax purposes. Often, rather than an expansion of service with technological advance, there has been a contraction, as firms retreat into safe ghettos of profitability. This has been choice, but choice resulting from severe pressures.

Often the workers have adopted a negative, reactionary stance. Consequently, there is a history in restrictive practices, low levels of output by workers, organizational failure and poor standards of work. The conventional answers are again close to the nub of the problem. The destructive dynamics of this self-indulgence in work have been to reduce the area of discretion which many companies could have to increase employment. We could follow back the history of 'the British disease' for several decades, but we would continually return to various forms of passivity, withdrawal and aggression which have their roots in the way workers are treated by the dominant group. Allen roots it firmly in public school and university educational values.[5] There are all kinds of intricacies to the long-term trend, but basically when attitudes operate which destroy the service dynamic of companies, employment suffers.

But there are structural aspects to the issue. Often companies have chosen, for reasons of profitability, directions with a false vision. In motorbike and car manufacture British companies have given priority to upmarket, profitable models and neglected, to their long-term cost, the provision of basic models for a mass market. They have ignored the needs of the dynamic but poor Third World markets in favour of the rich and sated ones of Europe. Government has placed a very high priority on supporting arms sales throughout the world, but a much lower one on aid-related exports. Meeting the needs of the old and handicapped in a non-exploitative way has scarcely been handled imaginatively by British companies. New areas of consumption — popular musical instruments, fast food, decaffeinated coffee, cassette recorders or nail-clippers have scarcely been dominated by British manufacturers. To have a vision for service is at least as important as technology, and this is where British companies have been strategically unaware.

Macroeconomic Policy

Historically there have been a number of phases of government policy with different and somewhat contradictory company strategies dominant in them. In the 1950s and early 1960s there were a series of Keynesian booms—in 1955, 1959, 1963, which coincided with elections. During this period, despite the advantages which Britain had in the post-war years, the emphasis, rather than being on a strong growth pattern, was on using labour as a variable either to increase or reduce output. There was a scepticism about long-term growth and an emphasis on meeting immediate demand. As long as domestic demand was healthy, there was a relatively subdued concern with overseas markets. In other words the immediate concern with year-to-year profits undermined a more strategic awareness of company development, especially for international markets, which were often used as a way of guaranteeing orders with shorter or longer delivery dates.

This was merely the beginning of a long period of oscillating macro-policy, which not only occurred with changes in government, but also, in the late 1960s and early 1970s, during a government's term. Changes in real interest rates, inflation rates, demand and exchange rates have been dramatic and unpredictable. The obvious result has been a distrust of long-term planning and investment, and a tendency of companies never to look beyond their present, rather insecure markets. Now, however, we face a much more drastic failure of macroeconomic policy, for the government of the

106

mid 1980s largely ignored its responsibility to encourage buoyant demand for goods and services especially in poorer areas. What does this mean? Is it just indulgent Keynesianism? No; that funds be channelled to those who through poverty have special needs for goods and services, so that the demand be effective, is a distributional responsibility which the Conservative Government has largely abdicated. They are not concerned with the redistribution of wealth and income. The consequence for industry has been that those with urgent needs for resources and services do not have the money to demand them, while those with money are sated and not generating employment. Later, we shall examine how crucial this distributional issue is to the failure of the Conservative governments of the 1980s to meet unemployment.

Company Development

British companies have also shown a lack of responsiveness to change. Partly, this was a question of technological traditionalism and a lack of sensitivity to market trends, but, more important, the adversarial company structure has often meant that change cannot be organized. Members of the work community are pulling in different directions, negotiations are tedious and drawn out, and all kinds of hidden agendas compromise the planning. There are dozens of examples where quite straightforward technological developments have been delayed through this lack of co-operation — car plant automation, flow-line ship production, containerization in the docks and on rail, automatic letter sorting and the like. The time period for responding to these changes could take twenty or thirty years if co-operation is absent, a far bigger delay than that caused by research and development. Delays in responding to change from this source have left British firms unable to adapt as they should.

Another reason has been the low level of investment. Without new capital on a substantial scale it is obviously less possible to reshape companies and industries. We have already seen institutional reasons in the financial sector for this failure. It is also related to the failure of companies to generate resources. Pollard, in *The Wasting of the British Economy*, identifies the stop-go policy outlined above, the deflationary policies of both the Labour and Conservative

107

governments after 1974, and the advent of North Sea oil with a high rate for the pound and the loss of jobs through low exports and import penetration as causes of this failure.[6] This analysis undoubtedly has substance, but equally important is the way in which lack of trust in a company prevents resources being ploughed back. It is normally seen as a prelude to the shareholders making a killing and induces stiffer demands for wages. Again one suspects it is the underlying untrustworthy relations which lie behind much of the failure to invest.

Market Control

Earlier we noted the way in which many companies are able to adopt a strategy towards the markets in which they operate. Traditional monopoly theory assumes that companies can trade off along the demand curve, but if the earlier suggestion that there is a demand band is correct, it is possible to increase prices in some markets without any immediate fall in sales. This is likely to happen in markets where the purchases are indispensable, either because they are components in a manufacturing process, or part of a composite consumer purchase. This kind of opportunistic inflation has tended to happen during periods of demand expansion, and it is clear, when it does, that its effect tends to reduce demand for other goods. It is a way of damping quite rapidly an expansionary trend. It certainly happened in the building industry in 1973/4 and is probably a widespread phenomenon which incidentally opens up the possibility of import penetration. If any expansion is going to be rapidly exhausted by opportunistic company inflation, it severely limits Britain's ability to conquer unemployment and shows again the need for an *internal* company control on inflation.

But the problem does not merely occur during periods of high demand. Over the last few decades there has been a massive concentration of ownership and control. Only in a minority of cases has the aim been greater productive efficiency. Some conglomerates have been diversifying to protect themselves against declining markets. Many other takeovers have aimed to extend the influence of a company over a market. Others have occurred to pick up cheap assets which can then be sold at a profit. Others have aimed to eliminate competitors. Others have been used by multi-national companies to gain a secure foothold in British markets. Whatever the particular form of acquisition, there tends to be one common market strategy which results. When demand falls, the companies are able to secure prices by eliminating part or all of the acquired company. That is, the companies go for maintained price at the expense of employment. When labour markets are closed to entry, and when salaries at the lower levels tend to be restricted, the inevitable result is a two-tier labour force with many of the lower tier unemployed.[7] This in turn raises the issue of the rights of the workforce within the decision-making structure of the company.

These points suggest ways in which the priorities and aims of companies have gone awry. In each instance we see the way in which the norm of service has been downgraded. Despite repeated structural failures, the business community has been happy to continue with the old familiar ideological model which gives them immediate personal security. As long as growth of sales continued and profits held up, they could operate with an indulgent employment policy, laxity in costs and short time horizons, although competition from abroad continued to be a problem. However, when in the 1980s demand was suppressed, these companies faced levels of acute failure, and unemployment followed in its train.

This failure is not entirely to be laid at the feet of the unions with their pay demands, restrictive work processes, slow response to technology and automatic adversarial stance. Nor even is it simply the fault of the managers. In many cases neither shareholders, management nor workers have had the long-term health of the company and its customers at heart. The whole value system in which corporate policy has operated has been fundamentally defective. Neither *laissez-faire* capitalism, nor its counterpart in economic theory, monetarism and neo-classical naturalism, provides the value base for enterprise, let alone any other aspect of economic life.

The Poverty of the Current Debate
There are reasons why the problems have not been tackled in these terms. One of them is the dogma which dominates political debate. It is the distinction between the private

sector and the public sector. The private sector, it is argued, is self-accountable free enterprise while the public sector is nationalized and accountable to the government. The only policy response to capitalist vices is nationalization and to the problems of nationalization it is privatization. Thus the silly see-saw of debate goes on, with the illusion that in 1984 British Telecom was 'privatized'. The reality, of course, is that all companies are public in the sense that they affect, depend on and are accountable to a large sector of the public. Indeed, the weakness of both Left and Right versions, nationalization and privatization, is that their pattern of accountability to the public is extremely weak—a remote plutocratic shareholders' meeting or a General Election. A much more direct pattern of accountability is needed which will finally eliminate this mythical private/public antithesis.

Another weakness is in the discussion of rewards. Wage demands are normally justified on the basis of parity with other workers, the rate of inflation or the supposed ability to pay. They are fixed in the sense that they do not carry some of the risks and uncertainties of the company, and they are 'demanded' on the adversarial basis that the maximum possible should be squeezed out of the employers. Meanwhile the shareholders receive widely fluctuating returns to their capital. Sometimes they receive massive windfall profits, especially if they also play the market 'correctly'. At other times the value of their assets declines. For neither is the relationship between their rewards and the situation of the company one of integrity. Yet because the deeper structural question of what the deserved rewards of the various contributors to the company should be is never discussed in principle, we finish with a shallow debate. We wait for the lamentations of the shareholders when the index takes a dive and hear the unemployed bemoaning their greedy colleagues, but nothing more.

Clearly, the concepts and categories of understanding in this debate are inadequate, especially in view of the crucial issues which face British business and industry, and the terms of it must be changed. But the new concepts must alter the framework in which business is viewed, and they must involve major changes in a company's internal structure which reflect more accurately what a company is meant to be.

The Internal Normative Structure of the Company

The company needs to be challenged at the level of its basic identity. At present it is a Board elected by the shareholders and accountable to them. The employees have no formal place within the structure of the company and it is implied that they are hired accessories who have no deeper commitment to the company. The model upon which this pattern is based is the eighteenth-century ownership of land as an inalienable right. It is amazing that few question whether this is the appropriate model to use for twentieth-century enterprises. Even when land is rented by tenants, rights have rapidly accrued to those who use it. Nor is it clear why the contribution of share capital should correspond to the purchase of land, since many of a company's assets result from ploughed-back funds. If we draw back from this fixation on persons owning things and consider what a company is in relational terms, we get some different answers.

First, if the *raison d'être* of companies is the service of the wider public who are its consumers, it is right that they should be represented within the structure of the company, so that the accountability of the company to the wider public can be explicitly recognized. A straightforward way of doing this would be to appoint consumer representatives to a third of the seats on the Boards of the larger companies. Their election, by registered consumers of the company's goods, would be no more complicated than the present election of shareholders' representatives. They would both make the company aware of its commitment to serve its customers and also provide a brake on the internal pressures to inflation. In an era when most major companies are able to shape the market strategy to a considerable degree, it is no longer any use relying on the external constraints of competition (or of government direction) to maintain sensitivity to the needs of the consumer. There should be an inner structural response to the norm of service which the representatives voted on by the company's consumers could provide.[8]

Second, it is time in Britain that the communal contribution of the workforce should be recognized within the company structure, as it has been in Germany since the Second World War.[9] The German model of shareholder/worker shared responsibility on the policy-making Board was developed in

111

principle as far back as 1918 when the Co-operative Association of German Industrial and Commercial Employers and Workers was formed. After the long tussle with more Fascist corporate attitudes, it emerged after the Second World War as an important structural commitment which has shaped the subsequent development of German firms very deeply. Employees could elect one-third of the representatives to the Board of companies with more than 2,000 employees since 1952, and in 1976 the Codetermination Act gave parity of representation on the Board to employees' representatives. Britain's traditional attitudes prevented this approach from being seriously considered until much later. By the mid 1970s enough concern had gathered to initiate the Committee of Inquiry under Lord Bullock.[10] It recommended the equal representation of shareholders and employees under what was known as the $2X + Y$ formula, but this recommendation ran up against two vested interests. First, the unions (and thence the Labour Party) were concerned about defending the power of unions, rather than employees, to bargain within companies. Second, the Conservatives (and the City) wanted to defend autocratic shareholder control of companies, and since the Conservative victory of 1979 the issue has been buried politically. They think at present that by curbing the activities of the unions they have re-established a viable pattern of control, but all they have done is to reassert another round of adversarial confrontation. As soon as the parameters of power change, the self-interest and partiality of the present pattern will become evident again. The answer remains the full incorporation of the employees into the structure of the company in recognition of their commitment to it. There are other ways in which the employees can share more fully in the company through flexible wages, profit and loss sharing and the contribution of capital, but the basic issue remains the recognition that the workforce is an integral part of the company at the highest level—on the Board.

This kind of reform, recognizing that a company is a community of workers and shareholders serving the public, would undermine the old propertied ideology of capital and open up a pattern of accountability which could operate in the public and private sectors alike. The tripartite board of shareholders, employees and consumer representatives would provide a suitable forum for a company to exercise stewardship in either sector. Indeed, when both 'public' and 'private' companies are so obviously remote from control by either elections or competition the only surprise is that more direct accountability has been held at bay for so long. There would be other consequences. Employees who had spent most of their life helping to develop a company would be less likely to see capital being arbitrarily moved off to another area. Control of multinationals would in part be retained within the nation, and takeovers would no longer be a matter of amassing sufficient shares. But the overwhelming change would be in the Board's corporate responsibility. It would at last be free to move beyond the destructive concern with self-interested profit-maximization which has done so much harm to British industry.

Notes

1. F. Engels, *The Condition of the Working Class in England* (Panther 1969), pp. 301–2.
2. M. Weber, *The Protestant Ethic and the Spirit of Capitalism* (Allen and Unwin 1977).
3. See, for example I. Kirzner *et al.*, *The Prime Mover of Progress* (IEA 1980) which largely has this self-congratulatory reflection on the role of entrepreneurs.
4. See R. Tawney, *The Acquisitive Society* (G Bell 1921) and G. Goyder, *The Responsible Company* (Oxford, Basil Blackwell 1961) for similar earlier statements.
5. G. C. Allen, *The British Disease* (IEA 1979).
6. S. Pollard, *The Wasting of the British Economy* (Croom Helm 1982), especially pp. 31–70.
7. Examined in the next chapter.
8. See *Christian Party Manifesto*, September 1974.
9. See H. Antonides, *Industrial Democracy: Illusion and Promise* (Toronto, CLAC, 1980) for a good survey.
10. Report of the Committee of Inquiry, Cmnd 6706.

8: The Professional Closed Shop

Shared Work

If the aim is work for all those who are able and willing to participate in the paid workforce, we should at least consider whether the work which is available is fairly shared. This is not a straightforward issue, because access to work depends on access to resources and on institutional arrangements. Even in a primitive society like that of ancient Israel, care needed to be taken that people had the resources with which to work. This was done through a long-term equitable distribution of land, but also in more immediate ways. The gleaning principle meant that when land or trees had been main-cropped other people could still work to gather the produce available. The Sabbath and other prescribed times of rest were ways of work rationing. To live in a society where work is shared and no one is either excluded from the possibility of paid work or enslaved to it, is a blessing which we notice more by its absence. Since work is so highly institutionalized in the contemporary economy, we need to ask whether the situation of those without jobs has something to do with the attitudes and policies of those in them.

The Two-tier Labour Market

We therefore look at the institutional context in which work takes place. Let us begin with a simple observation. On a straightforward naturalistic market model one would expect those who demand high wages to be unemployed and those who will accept lower wages to be employed, provided they are in the same market. Indeed, the exhortations all point in this direction. Yet the opposite is fairly universally true. Those with very high salaries sit comfortably in their jobs while the unemployed cannot get jobs at even subsistence levels of pay. The Chairman of ICI received a pay increase of 68 per cent at the beginning of 1985 without, it seems, running the risk of pricing himself out of a job. Here, indeed, is a mystery! Has naturalistic economics failed to live in the

115

real world again? How can this conundrum be explained? Using what Lakatos would call a degenerate form of explanation, we can rescue the semblance of a naturalistic market analysis. Skilled jobs, it is normally argued, create independent or segmented markets, which produce different conclusions from the one suggested above. If this is the case, we would do well to examine the relationship among these different markets.

In order to keep the analysis relatively simple, let us examine the possibility that there is a two-tier workforce in Britain, the top tier of which actually operates a strong policy towards work. Many people have both rewarding and worthwhile patterns of work and receive high rates of pay. The idea that pay is a compensation for the pain and disutility of work does not seem to fit their case. Although they may make occasional complaints and ritual groans about the burdens of work, the bulk of the professional, managerial and skilled workforce enjoy what they are doing and gain obvious rewards from their job. They have a high loyalty to their occupation, and their employers have a high commitment to them. Firms, public services and other organizations depend on a faithful, long-term motivated workforce, and through a variety of inducements persuade some of the workers to vest themselves in the enterprise or organization. Pension, pay, fringe benefits, status, enhanced leisure, power and flexibility all make the job more attractive and rewarding. Although servants have largely disappeared from the domestic scene, many upper-tier workers have access to personal servants during their working hours — secretaries, office staff, car care personnel, chauffeurs, cleaning staff and others are employed to serve them directly in their working needs. Of course, there is a pecking order in the upper tier and everybody has his or her price, but the overall result is to create a group of workers — the majority, perhaps — who are well paid, well looked after and secure.

This tier of workers does not face a trade-off between pay and employment. There are overall institutional constraints on pay like budgetary policy and levels of profitability, but generally, whatever is needed to keep them will be paid and quite a bit more besides. They are secure in their jobs because they have a powerful enough position within the organization

116

to limit entry and secure their own necessary contribution.

This leaves the 'dispensables'—dispensable because of lack of skill, possible fluctuations in levels of activity, technical developments and because the organization cannot afford to invest in these jobs. This lower tier, partly filled by women who will move in and out of the workforce and by those who fail to get a toehold in any organization, operates on much tighter price constraints: the 'going rate' is worked out to the last penny per hour. Moreover, organizations argue at this level—one does not know whether it is done with conviction—that more pay means fewer jobs. This distinction, between the upper tier and the 'dispensables', the insider and the outsider, is crucial to a proper understanding of employment failure. Let us relate it to the monetarist policies of the mid 1980s.

The monetarist recipe for job creation, as we have seen, is to bring wages down so that jobs may be created. If, however, the upper tier is cushioned by its power and engineered indispensability from any substantial impact on its wages, then clearly the wages of the 'dispensables' have to fall considerably to have any serious impact on overall costs. The proposed abolition of Wages Councils in the 1985 Budget was following this recipe. It is the dispensables who must work more efficiently, whose wages must bear the brunt of cuts in pay. This exposes the hypocrisy of much Conservative preaching on the way to fuller employment. Belt-tightening is limited to the lower orders; the Conservative-voting middle class continues to wear braces. But it also shows us that it is not sufficient to point at the double thinking of Conservative economic policy. Behind the ideology of monetarism lies a massive, complacent group of people who are looking after their own interests.

The Position of the Quasi-Professionals

Professionals have been the fastest growing sector of the workforce in recent years. Between 1971 and 1981 the number in education, welfare and health grew by one-third, while those in management, government, business, science and engineering grew by more than 20 per cent.[1] Attempts to halt this growth in the public sector (often on very generous terms of redundancy or early retirement) have hardly altered the trend. Focusing on professionals can, however, obscure a stronger trend.

For there is now a powerful argument for saying that a high proportion of workers are quasi-professionals — people with an exclusive training and expertise which allows them to fulfil tasks which others cannot do. They may have unique programming skills, can clone orchids, handle mechanical breakdowns, know a complex office system, can work on bank security systems or organize a recording studio. The exclusivity comes from three sources. The first is the ever-increasing complexity of the division of labour — many of us are and feel specialists. The second is education. It used to be seen as a ladder with a number of rungs at which one could step off. Although this element remains, the more useful image now is a fountain. At the top end education sprays out in all directions; it has become polytechnic. The third element is training on the job. Yet perhaps the exclusivity is overstated. If, rather than solicitors needing to bring the vast weight of their legal wisdom to bear on conveyancing, it is a relatively simple task, perhaps many of the quasi-professional tasks are not as exclusive as they claim. What the quasi-professionals may be doing is laying claim to the privileges of the professionals.

What are these privileges? Let us, for example, examine the position of doctors and nurses. The former are predominantly men and the latter women. In many ways nurses are treated as menials and servants; they are expected to make beds and do lifting. Doctors develop an aura of infallibility to maintain their unique authority to diagnose and treat patients and yet have a system to cover up their own mistakes. Never must their time be wasted by patients or anyone else. Everybody must queue to see them. At a lower level than the nurses is another tier of public servants, orderlies, cleaners and clerical staff, who are also expected to maintain the status of the doctors. In the area of midwifery, where women have training and expertise, doctors have harshly imposed their status to make sure that they have no rival authority. Clearly, doctors do not have a unique ability to diagnose athlete's foot or say when an X-ray is needed, but they are able to maintain an exclusive, well-paid, powerful position through the BMA and other sources of power.[2] What is true of this lucrative profession is reflected in others. For years primary-school teachers have held that parents could not properly teach their children to read, clergymen that they alone could lead worship, and architects that they had a monopoly on the aesthetic. There are many other groups which have to work harder to maintain the uniqueness of their skills. Some may just rely on wearing a white coat, or on keeping some information secret to themselves, or on asserting the right to vet the work of others. Yet the net impact is the artificial creation of professional indispensability as a route to job security and high pay. Put baldly, there is a direct relationship between job security and keeping others out.

This attitude has generated an industry of supporting structures. There are professional associations, the purpose of which is to erect hurdles, barriers and doors with handles only on the inside. Diplomas, conferences, courses and patterns of apprenticeship are constructed to help people jump over the hurdles and knock on the doors. In many cases the size of the hurdles has more to do with limiting entry than with the expertise needed to do the job. In some jobs, of course, it is not possible to erect hurdles because the tasks involved are not specialized, and here the unions come into their own to create exclusivity by rules. In some areas like printing and the media they have been highly successful; in others less so. Most, however, do not need unions.

One of the consequences of this pattern is that jobs are always pending. Waiting lists at hospitals become permanent. Social workers always have too many clients. Telephone engineers have a waiting list. Lawyers make sure that cases drag on. Especially during periods of depression the emphasis is on underperformance (provided exclusivity can be ensured) so that the occupational need is maintained. The quasi-professionals looked with amazement at the miners, who in 1984 were unwise enough to allow large stocks of coal to build up and then go on strike. The quasi-professionals make sure that there are too few of them to do the necessary work and that there is plenty of outstanding work to be done. Of course, what is being described here is only a tendency with many exceptions, but we cannot ignore the deep effects of quasi-professionalism on the economy and employment.

First, it has had a serious effect on efficiency. In crucial

119

sectors of the economy there has been quasi-professional underemployment which has prevented important tasks from being done. Design teams, which in Japan or elsewhere have become large dynamic units, have in Britain stayed small and secure. Sales units operated on a similarly inadequate basis. Social workers became too professional, clever and limited in number to cope with the scale of inner-city problems. Often the effect of these failures has been to lose jobs which depended on their efficient fulfilment. Another result has often been to put up the costs of other enterprises and reduce their scope and resources. Indeed, one way of regarding the present situation is not so much in terms of the public sector feeding off a smaller industrial sector, but professionals feeding off production and competitive workers.[3]

The second effect is directly on employment. Broadly speaking, a smaller and seemingly overworked group of quasi-professionals are employed at high rates of pay. The possibility of a larger and lower paid group of workers performing the tasks as well or better is ruled out by the preferences of the dominant group. Let us look at an example of this. Everybody knows that preventive medicine is better than remedial medicine. Why has almost nothing been done in the preventive direction? Because preventive medicine is a task for more and relatively unskilled workers which would undercut the demand for the present skilled élite. For this reason the BMA is unlikely to develop any strong strategy for preventive medicine. Similarly, the professionalization of social work has left a yawning chasm of needed care beneath the social workers. Millions of tasks are required to be done, but the pay and work priorities of the quasi-professionals preclude them. In the late twentieth century the privileged grip of professional exclusivism threatens to become every bit as strong as the medieval guild system and their restrictive practices as fierce. Or, to put it in other terms, the class war at the end of this century centres on professionalism, not capital.

The Technological Elite
The quasi-professional relation to work is a reactionary one in many ways; it is inherently protective. Yet there is another movement which is much more at the vanguard of current

120

economic development. In the 1960s Harold Wilson issued the call to mount the wave of modern technology and ride the crest into the future. His call has been echoed in the 1980s by Margaret Thatcher. Irrespective of the calls, there has certainly been a growth in high-technology occupations. Whether by automation, high-technology industry, micro-electronics, information technology or many other forms, technology is obviously affecting employment deeply. But how?

Conservative rhetoric points to the new high-technology industries and says to the young and the unemployed, 'This is the way forward. This is the future.' It may be for some workers — indeed quite a few, especially in the south — but many others will be excluded from this process. There are some trends which are quite likely. First, the job-creating potential of new technology is often greatest during its early development phase (unless costs drop significantly for other products). Second, where technology is held by monopolies, the normal result will be a smaller workforce, not lower prices. Third, most of the costs of technological change will be borne by the workers and their families through obsolete skills.[4]

Now this is not simply a matter of some being fortunate and others less so, for access to the high-technology area of employment also raises an important issue of justice in employment. We can examine this by looking at the capital/labour ratio of various jobs. If we look at the equipment people use, we find some workers are sitting on £50,000, others on £200,000 and others on £10,000,000 of capital in their day-to-day work. We note that none of the workers has *paid* for the capital and technology with which he works. It reflects no desert on him. Yet clearly, the difference between a worker who has very little capital to work with and one who has a great deal is important, especially (as was not the case during the Industrial Revolution) when the worker has some exclusivity in relation to the equipment. The difference in pay between a window cleaner, a lorry driver and an airline pilot is not just in their skills and training, but also in the fact that one has a bucket, ladder and chamois leather, another a £50,000 vehicle, and the third a £50,000,000 jet-plane to work with. Moreover, contrary to the claims of marginal productivity theory, it is not possible to dissociate

121

the contribution of the worker from that of the equipment. To say that the tractor driver ploughed so much of the field and the tractor did the rest is absurd. Evidently, these variations in the capital/labour ratio create an important issue of justice within the workforce. Through no virtue of their own, some workers are highly favoured while others face neglect and the inability to obtain the resources they need to work.

If we consider those who do not have access to capital and technology, they are clearly likely to suffer as dispensables and as the unemployed. They are the unenhanced workers who have little to sell but their labour. Conversely, others are able to bask in the resources they have at their disposal. Only a few, such as dentists and builders, actually purchase their own equipment. The high-technology middle-class groups assume this situation to be normal. Of course they have resources to work with. What is wrong with that? But the unfairness of this situation is patently clear, and many others feel the despair of being without resources. What fairness demands is either that the wage differentials induced by high levels of capital utilization be eliminated, or that there be a fairer distribution of capital and technological resources, or both.

We also need to consider the location of this new technology. If we ask what the key locational factors are today and until the end of the century, some rather unusual answers come back. One is that plants, research units, offices and laboratories are built where the high-technology workers want to live, that is predominantly in the south. Another is where there are flourishing markets, again in the south. A third answer is where there is a high-technological base — universities, polytechnics, other firms and research units. These are more widely spread nationally, but there are important areas of the north where they are noticeably absent. There are no universities in Derby, Sunderland, Middlesbrough/Stockton, Blackpool or Wolverhampton, but there are in Bath, Brighton, Colchester and Canterbury. These locational factors are not strategic in the old sense of needing nearby running water or being based on good coal reserves, but are the result of personal, family and educational preferences which all point south.

Nor will the market redress these trends, because a network

of interdependencies and inertia is being established which will keep this kind of job away from the north for the complete working lives of those who are entering the workforce now. The Conservative Government showed its indifference to this problem by lopping 45 per cent off its regional fund in 1984. The tide is ebbing from the north and each year the potential personal capital/labour ratios of school and college leavers north of the Wash is falling. They will be stranded in the economic mud of enterprise for most of their working lives, unless action is taken to meet this problem.

The State and the Workforce
Much of the provision of jobs is directly or indirectly related to the State, and here we face a rhetoric of concern which obscures what is really going on. At present the debate is conducted in terms of slimming the bloated public sector and increasing the efficiency of public-sector nationalized industries by making them more competitive. The impact of this process has been felt in the north and west Midlands. Beneath this efficiency drive remains a middle-class professional élite which continues to get many of the benefits of the public sector irrespective of the political debate. In some ways the Conservatives have challenged this group more than previous governments, and been labelled 'divisive' by its articulate members. Consider the ability of consultants to mount a campaign against the closure of their special unit in a hospital. They have publicity, clout, authoritative expertise, statistics and access to the decision-makers. By contrast consider the 'power' of those opposing the closing of job centres or sub post offices. Or look at the way in which the farmers have neatly secured a comfortable subsidized position within the EEC while the miners are castigated for asking for the same. This contrast has something to do with the fact that farmers have links with the Conservatives and predominate in the south, while the miners are linked to an ailing Labour Party and live in the north. The power given by the links with central government is crucial to the situation of many occupations in both the public and the private sector. This even extends to direct discrimination by the Secretary of State for Education against courses in Russian and the Social Sciences which he does not happen to like. Although one can

123

identify partisan trends, to their shame, with each government, the important question is whether central government decisions have a consistent direction in the creating and eliminating of jobs.

This is a difficult question, because so many hundreds of decisions and assumptions are involved in developing such a direction. It is also difficult because many areas of government decision-making are not assessed in regional and occupational terms. What in regional terms is the effect of government and NATO defence spending? Obviously, the direct effect of employment can be calculated—Aldershot, Portsmouth, the RAF and American bases, and other concentrations of forces personnel. The weight is certainly towards the south. But then there are the procurement and defence contract effects. Where do the contracts with British Aerospace, British Shipbuilders, Ferranti, GEC, Plessey, Rolls Royce, Royal Ordnance Factories, Westland, British Leyland, EMI, Hunting, Phillips, Racal, Dowty, Lucas, Marshall, Short, Sperry and Vauxhall get spent? Primarily it is in the south and reflects a Whitehall-centred view of the nation.[5] It is likely that this orientation is repeated many times over, reflecting nothing more sophisticated than a distance-from-London bias of indifference. There is no conspiracy or outright political partisanship, nor is it a matter of efficiency. It is just that the cumulative effects of privilege, self-interest and access to power work in a certain direction.

Let us approach the issue from a slightly different slant. If we exclude employees in manufacturing, distribution, agriculture and energy provision, we find that those employed in other services constitute 39.3 per cent of the employed workforce in the south-east, but only 26.8 per cent and 28.2 per cent in the east and west Midlands.[6] Why is this a significantly higher rate? Surely the need for the provision of services is not that much higher in the south-east? What is probable is that through all kinds of ways the funding of service employees is concentrated in the south-east and some other affluent areas. General practitioners per thousand of the population are more numerous, as are civil servants, university lecturers, farmers, customs officers, teachers and many others in 'service' occupations. Thus, funds are transmitted to the public services occupations in the south-

124

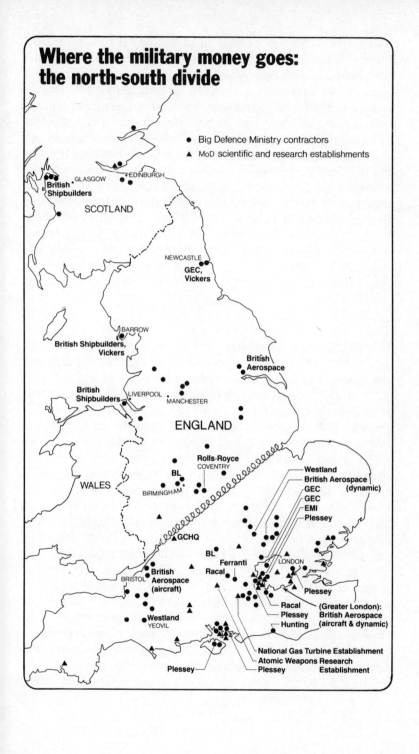

Where the military money goes: the north-south divide

● Big Defence Ministry contractors

▲ MoD scientific and research establishments

GLASGOW
EDINBURGH
British
Shipbuilders
SCOTLAND

NEWCASTLE
GEC,
Vickers

BARROW
British Shipbuilders,
Vickers

British
Aerospace

British
Shipbuilders
LIVERPOOL
MANCHESTER
ENGLAND

Rolls-Royce
COVENTRY
BL
WALES
BIRMINGHAM

GCHQ

Westland
British Aerospace
(dynamic)
GEC
GEC
EMI
Plessey

BL
Ferranti
Racal
LONDON

British
Aerospace
(aircraft)
BRISTOL

Plessey

Westland
YEOVIL

Racal
Plessey
Hunting

(Greater London):
British Aerospace
(aircraft & dynamic)

National Gas Turbine Establishment
Atomic Weapons Research
Plessey   Establishment
Plessey

east, which through normal local multiplier effects creates income for others in the area and helps to guarantee that this area remains affluent. What lies beneath this situation is a tacit set of agreements between governments and various pressure groups which make sure the government knows which side the bread should be buttered—normally the side closer to the current political establishment. It was interesting to note the grass-roots backlash from Conservative MPs and middle-class parents which firmly curtailed the Government's attempts to cut student grants in 1984/5. The strength of this power nexus in shaping the pattern of employment throughout the nation is considerable, and although there have been notable attempts in the past to discriminate positively in government employment policy, the overwhelming weight, especially since 1979, has been towards the south. For the government to claim neutrality in this area is not possible.

The Unions
It is strange that we should have spent so much time looking at the institutional framework of work without mentioning the unions, but this is because the unions are being drastically affected by these trends. Membership levels are falling below 10 million in a workforce of 26.5 million, but more notable is the way the old union ethos has collapsed. It had to collapse because it was compromised. On the one hand it has espoused the two-tier workforce model and some aspects of the professional model. The aim was to make union members exclusive and secure, if necessary by a closed shop, and to make sure that workers were employed irrespective of efficiency. The terms of reference were narrowly self-interested. The strategies adopted were indulgent and self-referential. In the 1960s and early 1970s the unions pushed up earnings and instant consumption. After 1974 they hoped for the status of privileged interest group in relation to the Labour governments and in the 1980s they have looked back to an expansionary Keynesianism which would give them more clout in the labour market. Meanwhile their membership has been fragmented by the two tiers, quasi-professionalism, the new technological élite and unemployment.

The old adversarial stance has guaranteed a largely negative attitude to work-creation within industry. Nor is there any sign of more co-operative policies opening up, for in many areas the resources of companies are so depleted that immediate protection of the workers becomes a more absorbing concern. The unions too have lost room for discretion and initiative. It seems clear that unless a different framework is created for the participation of workers in industry the old, tired, adversarial pattern will remain, weakened and perhaps intent on redressing its current defeat.

The Value of Work

We have been looking at the way in which work is seen from various self-interested perspectives. But something is going on here which many of us sense yet cannot identify. When work becomes self-centred (as it often does in the concept of 'career', which can be seen as little more than an extended ego-trip), the inner meaning and value goes out of the work. Its integrity as service is compromised. Yet it is precisely this ideology of self-interest, or, in the guise of naturalist economics, of individual utility maximization, which is continually being pushed as the basis of the contemporary work ethic. Initially, this approach seems attractive. We work for ourselves and this self-interest is the basis of an efficient and dynamic economy, so we are told. But in the longer term the ideology is revealed as a lie. Its self-seeking does not open up the value of work and service, but finds ways of exploiting work situations to the benefit of those who hold them, but to the destruction of mutual help. The process is slow and subtle, but in the end the ideology proves false. For a while self-interest can be manipulated to produce the local desired results, but in the longer term a service-ordered economy begins to deteriorate.

The process is not just personal, although people's lives are deeply affected by the spiritual emptiness of their work, but also structural. Work, which should be service, is something which is used to the cost of others. We have seen an underside to principled professionalism, which on the one hand upholds high standards of vocation, but on the other establishes, defends and expands its own privileges to the exclusion of others from work. Similarly, the top tier of the workforce uses power, capital, technology and training to its advantage to enhance its position and keep others out of work. It takes for granted the investment in training which it soaks up and the equipment and technology with which it works, to the extent that the plight of those without training and resources is simply not considered. The underlying attitude is a casual acceptance of the privilege which the upper tier of workers has accumulated to itself and an unwillingness to see how unfair this is to the dispensables. The emphasis, subtly at first but then more strongly, is on the minimum amount of work for the maximum amount of pay, which eventually makes other people's work more difficult. In the end the attitude produces graft and corruption; the estimated £1 billion involved in the Johnson Matthey Fraud Case in 1985 must be the tip of an iceberg of corrupt inefficiency which impoverishes most of us. These attitudes kill jobs. Clearly, one of the great needs is to break with this delusive ideology.

We begin again with the Christian principle that work has meaning within a frame of value which is basically God-given and relational. 'You shall love your neighbour as yourself' means work should be of value for my neighbour as for myself. It also means that I should value my neighbour's work and respect what he is prepared to offer. There is a false pride in the attitude which says, 'I have no need of you'. Therefore, the structures which lead the work of some to be valued highly and that of others to be disdained are distorted and in need of reform. People commit themselves to work in acts of faith: they are working out their lifelong contribution to the needs of others, and an investment of time, money and oneself goes into the process. We have already seen how privileged, unfairly so, many upper-tier workers are in this process. The value of work is incapable of being assessed merely in terms of immediate pay; commitment to a particular organization involves a level of trust different from that involved in selling a commodity, as is recognized by pensions paid to workers after they have ceased working for an enterprise. The old biblical terms of 'vocation' and 'calling' express what people often give in their work. It is the task which is asked uniquely of them as their contribution to the stewardship of God's creation and the service of others. We should therefore be committed to patterns of shared work and mutual service which allow the work of all to be given value (pay) and respect.

Constructing work for one another requires a radical redistribution of technical, capital, educational and organizational resources. The main impediment to this change is the protective reaction of the upper-tier workers. Without a change in their attitudes the political power to bring this about is simply not available.

Notes

1. *Social Trends* (HMSO 1985), p. 62.
2. Arguably, doctors have defended themselves against unemployment by moving heavily into high-technology medicine which saves far fewer lives than would alcoholism units, obesity clinics, stress units and anti-smoking units, but gives doctors status and jobs and an unassailable authority. They also create their own work through drug-dependence and symptom-relief. These are hard judgements, but it is easy for an established profession to be indulgent in evaluating its efficiency. See I. Illich, *Medical Nemesis* (Calder and Boyers 1975) for a statement of the medical ethos and its dependence-inducing character.
3. This fits with the growth of public and private sector health, educational and other professional services.
4. See K. W. Kapp, *The Social Costs of Business Enterprise* (Spokesman 1978), pp. 179—204 and DHSS, *For Richer, for Poorer? Cohort Study of Unemployed Men* (HMSO 1984).
5. Ministry of Defence, *Statement on the Defence Estimates* (1982).
6. *Census 1981 Key Statistics for Local Authorities: Great Britain* (HMSO 1984), pp. 58—71. Thirty-eight per cent of civil servants are in the south-east. See *Regional Trends* no. 20 (HMSO 1985), p. 93.

9: Families in Two Worlds

The Economic Importance of Families

In naturalistic economics the family is treated as a black box into which consumption goes, but which never has any independent effect on the economy, or responsibility towards it. Yet the opposite is the case. The modern family has immense discretion and a profound effect on the development of the economy. Its values and priorities shape many of the most important trends, and it has been one of the most dynamic sources of economic change over the last few decades. It has, of course, traditionally, been the domain of women, and consequently has been largely ignored by the male-dominated economics profession. However, there are other reasons why the family is ignored. Its internal economic activity involves no exchange, but is gift-based, and many economists in their pride have assumed that only exchange economics is 'real'. They also cannot handle what goes on inside the family in terms of maximization and prefer to see it from the outside as a calculating consumer box. In fact something like 30−40 per cent of all economic activity takes place within the family and economists have been more than foolish in ignoring it.

The family is not primarily economic; its central meaning is found in the relationships of marriage and procreation. Its norm is marital and parental love; people usually marry for richer for poorer, for love not money, and children are seen as a blessing and not an economic asset. It is the unit in which people experience birth, growth, intimacy and death, where they share work, have rows and hold things in common, all within a framework of unconditional acceptance. Whatever differences there may be in family values, it would be foolish to try to economize the family; the values are fundamentally social and only secondarily economic.[1] Yet the faith, values and direction of family life for this reason have a profound effect on the economy, for example, through a younger age of marriage, demand for a second car, requirements of privacy or a surge in overseas holidays.

For this reason the family has its own unique kind of economic activity. Issues of trading, desert, work, efficiency and scarcity take place within the context of the central love relationships of the family. Rather than maximizing their own satisfaction many parents experience 'going without for the children', and decisions are made on a family and marital basis rather than individually. Thus the quality of these economic activities is different from those of a company or bank, a point which economists who want to monotonize all economic decision-making cannot grasp. Most obviously, family activity is gift-based rather than depending on exchange; parents do not want paying for changing nappies.

These simple points immediately raise important issues. If the family has such an impact economically, has it affected employment? Are there changes in its structure, norms and faith direction which are reshaping the economy? Are economic policies undermining family life in ways which will bring serious long-term consequences? Let us briefly address some of these issues.

The Two-job Family and the No-job Family

The most obvious institutional change in relation to employment is the march of women into the paid workforce over the last twenty years.[2] Smaller families, more efficient homes, the growth of service jobs, the isolation of the nuclear family and possibly the fear of marital breakdown have led to a mighty exodus of women from the home. At one stage Patrick Jenkin, Secretary of State for the Environment in the first Thatcher Administration, urged women to go back to their homes to look after their families and give men more opportunity for employment. This is to give women the onus for the joint responsibility of looking after children, but the issue remains. Women seem to have boosted the workforce to the exclusion of men.

This rather sexist analysis misses the more important point. Women also participate more fully in the educational system, often successfully enough to become professional and high-technology workers. It is probable that upper-tier workers, male and female, marry one another. Marriage tends to take place during the period of college, university or early job training when there is a tendency for people of similar potential work experience to meet one another. Which of us does not know a two-teacher marriage? The general result is two-career marriages where both partners have roughly similar job prospects. For many of these families the process of establishing two substantial incomes may be a difficult one — involving postponing or limiting the number of children and coping with a demanding routine, but there is no doubt that dual-career marriages have emerged as a major phenomenon of the 1970s and 1980s. In a quarter of the marriages where the husband works full-time, the wife does as well.[3]

The flip side of this trend is obvious. It also means, if about the same number of jobs are available, that there are families where both the husband and the wife find it difficult to get and hold a job. They are both without the resources in terms of training and experience which lead to jobs. All kinds of factors such as poor education, low age of marriage, early conception of first child and lack of vocational training (if any) are likely to be shared by these couples. Most significant, however, is the area in which they live, which is likely to be depressed for both job-seekers. Although one would expect wives to compensate for the unemployment of the husbands, and doubtless many try, three-quarters of the wives whose husands are out of work are themselves either unemployed or economically inactive. The result is compelling: on the one hand, middle-class families with both partners commanding good jobs; and on the other, families where both partners are seen as lower-tier workers who are, or could be, unemployed.

There is another consequence of this pattern: the odd situation where a substantial proportion of the population feel rushed, under pressure, overworked and overcommitted, while another large group is yearning for things to do.[4] We do not know what the full economic consequences of this pattern are. How many dual-career couples are inefficient in their work, subject to periods of exhaustion and ineffectiveness, and end transferring domestic concerns to their workplace? There are no statistics, but most of us know subjectively, or through colleagues, of the way it pans out.

The problem can be illustrated with the help of a simple

model. If we assume that a full-time job takes up .5 of waking hours during the week and a child .2, then the following work and family patterns produce the commitments set out below. Above .7 denotes a situation of stress, below .4 one of inactivity. WD = weekday; WE = weekend; M = male; F = female.

| | | NUMBER OF CHILDREN | | | | | | | |
| | | 0 | | 1 | | 2 | | 3 | |
FAMILY PATTERN		WD	WE	WD	WE	WD	WE	WD	WE
1 Single working parent		.5	.0	[.7]	.2	[.9]	.4	[1.1]	.6
2 Single unemployed person		.0	.0	.2	.2	.4	.4	.6	.6
3 One working full time, other	M	.5	.0	.5	.0	.5	.0	.5	.0
at home. Split roles	F	.0	.0	.2	.2	.4	.4	.6	.6
4 One working full time, other	M	.5	.0	.6	.1	[.7]	.2	[.8]	.3
at home. Shared roles	F	.0	.0	.1	.1	.2	.2	.3	.3
5 One working full time. Other	M	.5	.0	.5	.0	.5	.0	.5	.0
half time. Split roles	F	.25	.0	.45	.2	.65	.4	[.85]	.6
6 One working full time. Other	M	.5	.0	.6	.1	[.7]	.2	[.8]	.3
half time. Shared roles	F	.25	.0	.35	.1	.45	.2	.55	.3
7 Two working full time.	M	.5	.0	.5	.0	.5	.0	.5	.0
Split family roles	F	.5	.0	[.7]	.2	[.9]	.4	[1.1]	.6
8 Two working full time.	M	.5	.0	.6	.1	[.7]	.2	[.8]	.3
Shared family roles	F	.5	.0	.6	.1	[.7]	.2	[.8]	.3
9 Neither employed	M	.0	.0	.0	.0	.0	.0	.0	.0
Split family roles	F	.0	.0	.2	.2	.4	.4	.6	.6
10 Neither employed	M	.0	.0	.1	.1	.2	.2	.3	.3
Shared roles	F	.0	.0	.1	.1	.2	.2	.3	.3
11 One employed half time.	M	.0	.0	.2	.2	.4	.4	.6	.6
Split role	F	.25	.0	.25	.0	.25	.0	.25	.0
12 One employed half time.	M	.0	.0	.1	.1	.2	.2	.3	.3
Shared roles	F	.25	.0	.35	.1	.55	.2	.65	.3

Stress ☐ Inactivity ——

Put crudely, the thesis is that the movement has been from number 3 with two children to either 5, 6, 7, 8 or 1 with two or fewer children, or 9, 10, 11, 12 with two children or possibly fewer for economic reasons. Both stress and poverty could be reasons for restricting family size; the declining birthrate has coincided with the emergence of this pattern.[5]

How do we meet this situation? The problem arises over the full-time definition and structure of most jobs. This is the result of pressure from employers, unions and professional groups. The former want to maximize the work output per employee, especially in view of the overheads involved in employing full-time workers, and the latter want to maximize pay and other benefits. The result has been a rigid full-time package which leaves many people in 7 or 8, with stressful lives (or not doing their job properly) but with massive incomes.[6] All the institutional pressures have pushed in this direction. Nevertheless, provided people were prepared to take a realistic cut in pay, probably slightly more than proportional, it would be possible to develop 4/5 or 3/5 working patterns which spread the work much more effectively. This could happen on a large scale if people saw beyond making maximum incomes an absolute priority. Changes in the costs to employers of full- and part-time employment could encourage the process. Only if this fundamental step in work reallocation is taken will the two-job and no-job family patterns begin to crumble.

However, this is not simply a matter of the attitudes of families and employers changing. The Government, with its present policy of moving taxation from direct to indirect forms, is encouraging this pattern. Lower income tax does not so much encourage the lower-tier worker to find a job as encourage the upper-tier family to find two. The taxes on expenditure tend to be regressive, leaving the unemployed in more acute poverty. In view of the fact that a second full-time job is a privilege in our society it is arguable that it should be taxed. An employment tax charged to the employee, not the employer, in the situation where the job was the second or more full-time job in the household (combined with the right marriage and dependants' tax allowances), or higher income tax rates on joint earned income, would reflect the fact that these jobs are a boon often obtained to the disadvantage of others in considerable need. This, of course, would require a volte face in the philosophy of the present Government, which sees these issues in terms of individual incentives to aspire to high rewards.

135

At present we have the situation where highly trained husbands and wives who have experienced the best of British education and training (largely provided free) are bringing in massive combined incomes, while other couples struggle for part-time jobs. Unless the rules of the jungle apply, this is hardly just.

The Pattern of Family Employment
We have looked at the family and paid work, but the family economic system, which operates on gift relationships rather than exchange ones, has its own internal pattern of employment, overemployment and underemployment. The domestic economy can distribute work and time in a number of different directions: paid employment, child care and contact, house and garden work, house investment, voluntary work, social leisure and passive leisure.[7] Each of these needs to be taken into account at various stages of the family life cycle.

What is happening to the pattern of family employment? One development which is little taken into account is the decline in voluntary work. The significance of voluntary work for the economy is often ignored, yet it may amount to 10 per cent or more of the work done outside the family. Its value is that it allows needs to be met without requiring the resources of pay for the services rendered. It is thus one of the most flexible forms of economic activity. Yet, especially with the move of middle-class women into the paid workforce, the amount of voluntary work has declined substantially (except during the miners' strike in 1984, when it effectively took over the local economy). This has both made extra demands of the public welfare agencies and removed resources especially from the old, those with young children and the sick. With the cutbacks in various welfare provisions we therefore have an area where work is needed, but the pattern of funding to generate the work is underdeveloped.

Another trend which is quite firm is away from child care and contact and towards paid employment in the two-job families. Mobility, especially during early married life, and lack of contact with grandparents, probably reduces the quality of care both for children and the old. Things which children can learn quickly and competently when they are

136

young may well take much time and expense to teach them when they are older—simple things like respect for persons and property, patience, and how to sort out quarrels. Here we see another area where more work is needed; we have one of the lowest levels of nursery provision in Europe despite the high participation of mothers in the workforce. Daily we see evidence of the millions of pounds that these failures may cost and have cost in the form of vandalism, juvenile crime, violence and poor learning patterns.

Conversely the unemployed are able to spend more time with their children and are knowing some of the blessings of so doing. However, much of the trade-off is between unemployment and passive leisure. Other possibilities are not open and the defeat and lack of resources that follow from being without a job leave them little alternative but to withdraw into television and video watching. Contrary to what is sometimes asserted, these unemployed people do not have the resources to make strategic choices about unpaid family work. They cannot maintain their homes, educate their children or undertake work in the community without help. Clearly, the Manpower Services programmes are moving into this area, but much more potential communal work is still available.

Family Inflation and Deflation

Once we move away from the crude monetarist view of inflation it is possible to see ways in which various institutions contribute to higher prices. For example, families practise various levels of thrift. Some shop around and spend much time over purchasing. Others buy with facility at almost any price; they have a wide demand band. Given the trends we have already examined, two-career families, short on time and with substantial funds and credit, will purchase with less care. Indeed, they will want to shop in buy-all supermarkets which eliminate the possibility of competition. Just as one notices astronomical prices when tourists are throwing their money around, so there will be a tendency for inflation in areas where the affluent live and purchase, especially if they regard these purchases as 'necessities'. Area-based inflation becomes noticeable. Retailers who can easily make profits on high-demand and upmarket commodities move into the affluent areas.

When families decide to move, the transmission of their purchasing power, especially in relation to fixed assets like housing, becomes very marked. Between 1971 and 1981 roughly 100,000 people moved out of Birmingham, Manchester and Liverpool.[8] If we say they constituted about 25,000 owner-occupied households with £10,000 of capital each (a conservative estimate), then these three cities experienced a drain of £750 million during the decade, depressing the value of the assets of those who remain. Conversely, property prices move up to a multiple of two or more in job-rich areas, effectively excluding those from the depressed regions. The poor in the area face high prices and find their consumption needs ignored, and are slowly pushed out.

As well as these market and geographical effects, families also have important temporal effects on inflation. With the lax financial constraints following Competition and Credit Control and the Heath Government's push for growth in 1972−3 many families learned that to borrow and purchase assets was a quick route to personal affluence. Domestic credit for the purchase of houses, land, antiques, art, second homes, unit trusts and other family investment markets opened up. The effects of this family credit expansion and speculation were threefold; it directed funds away from long-term capital creation, poorer families lost out and the young found themselves in a vulnerable situation. A similar pattern existed in the 1920s when a period of high borrowing and inflation during the First World War was followed by an era with high real interest rates and good returns for the rentier class. At that time many of the younger generation had been killed. Now they face the results of earlier consumer credit and underinvestment in the form of depression and high real interest rates. To meet these financial burdens many of them aim to keep both partners in full employment, even when the children are very young, and limit the size of their family to cut down on their financial obligations. So the intergenerational reaction continues and the middle-aged have a substantial charge of unfairness to meet from the young who now see them protecting the value of their financial assets with tighter money and City-orientated policies.

An interesting aspect to this issue is the rate at which the older generation transmits its wealth to the younger members of the community. Especially with the inflated value of some assets, it is probable that the old are considerably more wealthy relative to the young than has occurred at other periods of our recent history. Some of the young, with poor employment prospects and relatively few assets, are economically weak in terms of their earning potential. If they come from families which missed out on the capital gains of the early 1970s, they are in a very weak position. It may be that some more affluent families are very slow at transmitting wealth to the next generation. Information is extremely limited, but the pattern is likely to be an arbitrary one which leaves many young families bereft of resources at a crucial time. Hereditary wealth is still largely seen as an absolute right to property along the lines of eighteenth-century landed philosophy and the incidence of wealth taxes on affluent middle-aged families has declined. The biblical emphasis on the stewardship of property and on the provision of livelihood for all suggests that one of the aims of a wealth tax should be the transmission of funds equitably from the old to the young.

The Family and Consumption

The traditional concern of Keynesian analysis was with the propensity to consume out of income. We are now in a position to present a more institutionally aware understanding of this important aspect of the economy. The two-job/no-job family pattern has important effects on consumption. Since the marginal propensity to consume is lower for high-income groups, the movement to two-job families will tend to depress consumption. The extent is probably even greater, for two-job families do not have the time to spend what they earn. They are also more likely to spend on imports — foreign holidays, cars, hi-fi, consumer durables, cameras. This points to a problem of domestic underconsumption. The two-job families have too much to spend with little time to do it, and the no-job family has urgent needs but no funds. This suggests that there may be a structural problem of underconsumption from the family, and there are other reasons for believing this is so.

The British population is getting older. We all know that the proportion of the population over retirement age is

139

increasing and that the birthrate has fallen below replacement rate. This is likely in the longer term to lead to a lower ratio of able-bodied workers to the dependent population of old and young, but it is also likely to affect expenditure. How? There is one hypothesis which posits that people view their consumption according to a lifetime plan. On this view, saving, often in the form of pensions, is built up during the working life to provide funds for the dissaving era of old age. This would imply that we are presently in an era of relatively high personal saving which will be superseded by one of dissaving. Although this pattern is important, and the demand for winter cruises probably will not decrease, there is an alternative view which is more compelling.

The old have accumulated most of the property and chattels which they need for living. If anything, they begin to reduce their needs in terms of space, transport, food, clothes and consumer durables. It is more than possible that those who have been saving, by habit and for security, will continue to do so as their consumption tails off. The alternative scenario is therefore one of satiation, not just for the old, but also for those who have established their homes and consumer-durable base in middle age. At the other end of the age spectrum the numbers of those moving into the home and family building era is likely to be reduced (and a proportion of these will have no jobs and few resources). If the low birthrate is related to levels of divorce, the fear of divorce, the availability of abortion and the need for independent women's employment, it is possible that this reduction in the birthrate will be severe. The conclusion which follows is that, without changes, we are likely to encounter an era of reduced effective demand with its inevitable effect on jobs. On this view, especially with the severe limitations on the ability of the chronically poor to spend, underconsumption is likely to be a major problem.

Keynes focused on a falling marginal propensity to consume with higher incomes, but there are ways in which this basic insight needs to be elaborated with respect to the wealth of families. Wealth has increased in significance considerably since the time of Keynes; at that time families might have possessed something like their annual income in wealth. Now it would be four or more times as much. Obviously, it is likely

140

to be important in shaping all kinds of consumer responses.

But how, broadly, does wealth affect the situation? First, we need to make a distinction between consumption wealth (i.e. assets which retain value but are primarily held for reasons of personal satisfaction) on the one hand, and income-generating wealth on the other (which we shall consider in the next section). Consumption wealth has been more widely spread in the post-war era, and at certain periods generated much economic activity in the form of housebuilding, car production and the sales of consumer durables. Not only is this activity likely to diminish with smaller population growth, but the emphasis in consumption wealth has changed. Much of it is now positional; it involves living in a certain area, which may affect housing prices by a multiple of 3 or 4, owning antiques or sending children to exclusive schools. Often the acquisition of consumption wealth has also through market forces put funds in the hands of the established wealth-holders; one thinks of the movement in building-land prices. This kind of consumption wealth is job-degenerate, doing nothing to create jobs.

Thus we see that both the income and wealth effects generated by contemporary family life are likely to issue in patterns of underconsumption, more serious in some areas, but still quite ubiquitous. The situation reflects that of the 1870s and the 1930s. Of course, through easy credit it would be possible to offset this structural tendency for a while, but it would need this kind of compensating policy if the underlying inequalities of income and wealth are not corrected. Conversely a nation is blessed when its resources are more widely shared among its citizens.

Family Investment Policy

Families are, of course, one of the biggest sources of investable surpluses in the economy. The strategy which a family adopts in its investment policy is thus crucial to the development of the economy, and has been at every period since the Industrial Revolution when certain families like the Bridgewaters and the Wedgwoods provided the dynamic for growth. During most of the subsequent period, families transmitted funds to the local economy through banks, personal loans, direct investment or by ploughing back funds into assets. Some personal wealth found its way to the City and trade, but most of it was quite tightly bedded in the local economy. Of course, few families were actually rich enough to have the surplus available to invest, and those who were often held it in land and other traditional forms of wealth. By contrast, one amazing thing about the early industrialists is their asceticism, the way they committed money to industry and did not spend it on themselves. We cannot look properly at the earlier investment patterns of families, but at least it is evident how different the strategies have been at various periods. What is the pattern now?

First, the amount potentially available for investment has expanded radically. Many people now have funds surplus to their more immediate needs. As we have noted, the high ratio of wealth to income is an important new phenomenon, and it is more widely spread, although many still have few resources beyond what is immediately coming into the home each week or month. However, much of this wealth is held as consumption wealth—owner-occupied housing, cars, caravans, second homes, furnishings, boats, jewellery and antiques. Indeed, compared with, say, Japanese families, the British seem to be very ready to move into consumption wealth rather than income-generating or investment wealth. When we focus on the latter category the pattern of ownership is very much more concentrated. There has been a decline in the taxation of wealth since the early part of the century which has left large fortunes to accumulate. It seems that the rich still marry the rich, and those who can choose when they will sell or buy have had a considerable opportunity to make more wealth. If it were possible to construct an index of the profits made through fluctuations in prices relative to those made through the production of goods and the provision of services, the ratio would probably be high during the last twenty years. If we add in the lowered rates of taxes for the rich in the Thatcher administrations, and tax avoidance, it is probable that there is a significant concentration of wealth and the income derived from it, in a relatively small, although expanding, sector of the population. The figures for distribution of wealth are difficult to interpret, but, for what these figures are worth, the Inland Revenue has reported 10 per cent of the population over eighteen owning 56 per cent of the marketable wealth. This suggests that the concentration is substantial.[9]

There is an exception to this pattern. Pensions are income-generating wealth, and they, together with various forms of insurance, are increasingly taken up by a larger proportion of the population. What about this vast concentration of 'income-generating' wealth administered by the institutions? As we saw in the chapter on financial institutions, the use of this wealth tends to be job-degenerate. Because the institutions are concerned with a reliable future income flow, they only engage in what we shall call secondary investment, i.e. investment in already established capital, and little flows into job-creating capital.

If we return to those with whom income-generating wealth is mainly concentrated, we have to acknowledge that a certain motive tends to dominate their orientation to their wealth. It is the straightforward desire to maximize their wealth and income in a secure and unproblematic way. For most people in and around the City the value is so unquestionable that even to state it is to dishonour the dogma. Yet the question remains as to whether this motive leads funds to be channelled into the old-fashioned primary investment which creates jobs? The answer to this is probably a disappointing one. A lot of the time this motive signposts funds to rentier-type asset holding. Property, overseas assets, government stock, building society loans, established shares and other forms of asset which give a secure but lucrative source of revenue are the preferred direction of these funds.

Thus the normal pattern is for pension funds, insurance companies, building societies, unit trusts or some other institutional channel to become the recipient of the funds, with no other requirement than that they will produce a satisfactory rate of return on the investment. Not only is this direction conservative, but it also gives the institutions which handle these funds a brief which says 'Play safe with our savings'. The family becomes a willing pawn in the whole process, and the centralized institutions' use of the funds determines the actual pattern of investment. In contrast with the earlier pattern the present one is cut off from the locality, from local employment prospects and from the possibility of making decentralized investment decisions. Family policy allows our financial institutions to be incapable of responding

143

to many of the job-creating investment opportunities which are around. Passivity reigns.

One of the main reasons for this change is the lack of care which surplus-generating middle-class families show in using their funds. Patterns of automatic accumulation set in which take little or no account of the use to which funds will be put. This abdication of responsibility ignores the fact that ten middle-class families can easily, directly or indirectly, employ a person full time. The possibilities of family initiative in job creation and investment are limitless, provided they see beyond a rate of return on money as the only goal in using their surpluses.

Family Breakdown

Another way in which the family is profoundly affecting the economy and the pattern of employment is through its breakdown. When between a quarter and a third of all marriages disintegrate, there have to be serious consequences. One is waste through the duplication of resources. The 'useless' expenditure induced by marital breakdown includes legal costs, the duplication of housing, cars, consumer durables, costs in terms of stress and work inefficiency and many other items impossible to quantify. If we consider the costs involved in changing the stock of housing needed, we have to recognize that an extra burden of £2,000 million plus (at a guess) is being carried for that alone. When we note that the unemployed are more likely to experience marital breakdown, we can feel the personal depths of despair involved. What problems this is creating for the next generation, and what economic burdens will go with them, we scarcely dare think.

However, there are other important consequences of this pattern of breakdown. The *fear* of breakdown imposes on many women and men the belief that they must independently be able to earn their own living, and these days this means actually having a job. The change in the conception of personal security from the old pattern of marital troth 'for richer, for poorer' is helping create the extra demand for employment among women especially which is part of the current picture. The tragic lack of peace in marriage again produces a destructive economic consequence, as many women do more paid work than possibly they would really want to.

Breakdown has led, and is likely to lead, to a reduced birthrate. This creates a decline in demand, initiative and dynamism, and eventually a fall in the employed/dependent ratio. It reduces employment in areas such as education concerned with helping and training the young, and is likely to add to the pattern of underconsumption mentioned earlier in this chapter. Clearly, all of these factors need to be taken into account in any far-sighted approach to employment.

Poor Families and their Needs

Unemployment is usually seen as an externally imposed condition, something which results from the operations of the market economy with which the family then has to cope. Certainly, it does profoundly affect the family economy, but usually more is going on than this view implies. Families are living organisms, and when they suffer, recovery is a slow and difficult process. It can take several generations. Let us look at what many of the unemployed go through.

Unemployed people are likely to have been earning well below the average wage before they lost their job. They are likely to be married to somebody whose market employment prospects are not too strong. The family resources in terms of property, education, experience, scope and contacts may well be limited. Whatever assets the family has are likely to be severely depleted and to leave the next generation with little to help them start out. Poverty, as numerous studies show, is not just economic, but psychological, social, educational, spatial (whether domestic or geographical) and linguistic. It is evidenced in noise levels, lead levels and numbers of handicapped children. Vandalism and environmental decay will be more prevalent in poor areas, whether as a result of the detritus of commuters or inner-city youth cultures. The inescapable conclusion is that many who face unemployment do it from a position of weakness, especially if they are young.[10]

The other side of this situation is the poverty which results from unemployment. The income of the out-of-work person usually falls to about half the previous level. If the car has to go, getting around is more difficult and time-consuming, and making ends meet takes up more time as every bargain is hunted down. Being out of a job means a quick loss of skills and employability. Those who leave school jobless fail to pick up many of the basic skills needed for work. The family unit experiences a deterioration in its mobility. All too often this despair induces irritation, sickness, depression, withdrawal, suicide and other forms of family tragedy which those outside the family can scarcely guess. These are costs which should rank high in our macroeconomic calculations.

We note finally that jobs cost money, especially when people are starting in them. Because the neo-classicals regard work as a disutility, the idea that people invest in their jobs has largely been ignored. But they do—in terms of study and training, means of travel, clothing and, in the case of manual work, more food (there is always a good butcher in a mining community). These threshold costs face the unemployed, together with the direct costs of searching for a job and climbing over the poverty trap. Thus many families face a confluence of circumstances which help keep them unemployed, especially in job-barren areas. It is no good assuming that family initiative will solve these problems when so much is stacked against the unemployed.

Children also learn about work primarily in their family. This is shown by the tenacity of employment patterns from generation to generation. They learn work habits, organization, commitment, reliability, skills and pride in their work from their parents, and the absence of this opportunity is a severe loss. There is not normally more hope out on the streets either. For some the more sordid activities of crime, alcoholism and drugs take root and make the situation even more insoluble.

Conclusion
The way in which the institution of the family structurally affects the economy is evident. But if these changes feed the pattern of unemployment, they need to be met. The two-job/no-job polarization should be met by a transfer of training and resources. The underconsumption profile needs to be corrected. Passivity in the use of family investment should be remedied, and the restoration of viable family economic units needs to be encouraged as soon as possible. In the face of this family poverty it is not uncommon to hear remarks that

throwing money at problems does not solve anything. A big part of the problem is the way unemployed and poor families have had money leeched out of them. On the whole they need transfusions of money and resources to regain health. Much of it is their due. We are not yet in sight of generosity.

Notes

1. This view is fundamentally opposed to the approach of G. Becker, *A Treatise on the Family* (Harvard University Press 1981) which treats all family decisions as individual maximization problems. For a fuller sociological treatment of the structure of marriage and the family see A. Storkey, *A Christian Social Perspective* (IVP 1979), pp. 134−6, 196−247.
2. More particularly married women, and a markedly different pattern from the more stay-at-home women of the Netherlands, Italy and Belgium. *Social Trends* no. 12 (HMSO 1982), pp. 63−4.
3. See *Social Trends* no. 15 (HMSO 1985), p. 26 and G. Thomas and C. Zmroczek 'Household Technology: The "Liberation" of Women from the Home?' in P. Close and R. Collins (see note 10), pp. 101−28, and also R. and R. N. Rapoport, *Dual Career Families* (Penguin 1971) and *Working Couples* (Routledge and Kegan Paul 1978) for an interesting comparison.
4. See S. B. Linder, *The Harried Leisure Class* (Columbia University Press 1970) for one side and L. Fagin and M. Little, *The Forsaken Families* (Penguin 1984) for the other.
5. For a more personal description of the kind of issues involved in this model see S. Wallman, *Eight London Households* (Tavistock Publications 1984).
6. See S. Edgell, *Middle-class Couples* (George Allen and Unwin 1980), pp. 72−89.
7. Covered in depth in R. Pahl, *Divisions of Labour* (Oxford, Basil Blackwell), and S. Dex, *The Sexual Division of Work* (Wheatsheaf 1985).
8. Census 1981, *Key Statistics for Local Authorities* (HMSO 1984), pp. 6−7.
9. *Social Trends* no. 15 (HMSO 1985), p. 90.
10. See N. Madge (ed.), *Families at Risk* (DHSS/HEB 1983); M. Moynagh, *Making Unemployment Work* (Lion 1985), ch. 1; T. Walter, *Hope on the Dole* (SPCK 1985); J. Popay, 'Women, the Family and Unemployment' in P. Close and R. Collins (eds.), *Family and Economy in Modern Society* (Macmillan 1985), pp. 174−91; and G. Allan, *Family Life* (Oxford, Basil Blackwell 1985), pp. 144−66.

10: The Welfare State

The Reform of What?

In 1985 Norman Fowler, Secretary of State for the Social Services, began the most systematic reform of the Welfare State since the time of Beveridge.[1] But by 1986 the zeal had gone out of the campaign and it was dying the death of many qualifications. What was being reformed? The 'Welfare State' is the name we give to the collection of central government activities which aim at meeting the social problems arising in the economy and in society at large. This will do for an initial definition, but it raises more questions than it answers. Does the Welfare State expect to remedy these problems? Is taxation as well as benefits within its ambit? How is it funded? What position does it have in relation to unemployment? We could rush at these questions and search for answers, but there is a stage we need to tackle first. Until the various meanings given to the Welfare State by different political groups in our society are articulated, we will not be in a position to see why it operates the way it does and why the debate is so clouded.

It is possible to discern five major models of the Welfare State which give rise to different principles of operation and diverse responses to problems which crop up. Although in practice they are superimposed on one another, they help explain the inconsistencies in the operation of this aspect of government and the diverse attitudes adopted in meeting unemployment. Let us examine each of these models in turn. We shall then look at some aspects of the organization of welfare, and the relationship of the Welfare State to other aspects of the State and local government. It will emerge that the inconsistencies of approach to welfare are further muddied by these factors. Finally, the model which most faithfully accords with the main biblical imperatives will be looked at in more detail.

Model 1: *Laissez-faire* Paternalism

This approach is based on the classical and neo-classical view of economics criticized in earlier chapters. On this view

149

the economy functions as a natural mechanism which automatically leads to good results. People are expected to operate independently on the basis of self-interest through patterns of self-help and healthy competition. For those who are independent, the State has no welfare role, and to create one would in the end merely infringe their freedom. However, if for any reason people become dependent, the State must step in to help the casualties on the basis of proven overt need. The help must be accompanied by strict rules to avoid abuse and prevent the dependent group becoming a burden to the State, and the help must in no way discourage people from reachieving their independence. Essentially the State's involvement is seen as the minimum consistent with what is needed to meet people's personal needs.

This approach has a long history. It was present in the Poor Law and was made more rigorous by liberal utilitarianism during the workhouse era. Its chief spokesman was Edwin Chadwick.[2] He began from a belief in self-interest as the dominant motive in human action. Welfare provision was a problem when it acted as a disincentive for the able-bodied to work. For the Poor Law to be efficient it needed to provide incentives to get people back to independent living. In this way the evils of indolence and waste would be avoided. It was dominant through the long period of the Victorian Poor Law, an era when taxes were astonishingly low, and has continued to the present day in the means-tested benefits which provide the most basic level of present Social Security. In 1966 the old National Assistance Board was renamed the Supplementary Benefits Commission, and throughout the late 1960s Labour politicians fought over the introduction of means-tested help to families.[3] But Family Income Supplement was introduced and the tests have stayed with us. Although the approach has become more humane than it was in the nineteenth century, still the procedure is forbidding and many benefits are not taken up. Now no blame need be attached to the person who is forced into dependence, yet the underlying assumptions rule that the natural and normal state to which all people should aspire is independence and self-help. Benefits are for the abnormal poor.

Unemployment is one of the most obvious ways of moving into dependence. So the unemployed need basic support until they are able to obtain a job in the labour market again. It is not the task of the Welfare State to help provide the job, for that will happen through market forces. Because the approach is based on individualism and self-interest, the position also presumes no necessary relationship between the unemployed and the broader population. It is the job of the State to cope with the unemployed until they find work like everybody else. The main problems of this approach are twofold. First, it ignores the way in which 'market forces' include a range of decisions taken by other members of the community which move people into unemployment. The arelational economic base is fundamentally misleading. Second, it does not face the issue of helping the unemployed to put together the resources they might need to obtain a job.

Finally, we note that this approach produces a quite marked dividing line. Either people are dependent or they are not. The line can be drawn quite accurately on one side or the other of citizens to decide whether or not they need support.

Model 2: Individual Insurance

This second view is also a product of individualism. Everybody, it argues, faces the possibility of various vicissitudes in life, and it is part of a normal, wise response to this situation to try to protect and cover oneself against them. With the minimum of co-operation it is possible for people to provide themselves with various forms of insurance against these problems. Indeed, this is the best way of preventing the move into dependence discussed above. For the individual establishes a contractual relationship with the insurer and pays his contributions, and therefore has a right to receive any benefits which become due to him. If everybody is adequately insured on this basis the problem of dependence is fundamentally solved. The past contributions of the various individuals provide the funds available for benefits.

This approach developed most strongly in the mid and late nineteenth century as the Friendly Societies got under way, but it was modified in a number of ways which we need to note. First, a difficulty arises with private, self-interested insurance. Those who are evidently less likely to need benefits, can, if they insure as a bunch, achieve much more favourable terms of benefit, while those who are most likely to need benefits find their rates unfavourable. Universal, national insurance required by the State overcomes this problem. All contribute and there is a complete averaging-out of risks. This, by and large, was achieved by Lloyd George's National Insurance Bill of 1911, which was fiercely opposed by the supporters of Model 1. At the same time another development took place. The insurance was not just individual, but also involved contributions from the employer and the State; it was moving towards social insurance, our third category.

Individual insurance had a potentially wide scope. It raised the question of what needed to be covered by insurance. Sickness, unemployment, disability and maternity benefit were certainly on the list, but what about other slightly less basic categories of need? They could be privately insured. And if the minimum provisions were met, was it not better to leave private insurance to pick up particular wants which people had over and above these basic needs? Recent Conservative thinking has certainly subscribed to this view.

Unemployment is seen as that which the individual can insure against. Some problems are created by those who, on entering the workforce, have not been able to establish sufficient contributions to qualify, and there are also times when the demands on the scheme are greater than the historic contributions can meet; this problem occurred with unemployment insurance after the First World War, and the State had to step in to provide direct relief. Also, this approach does not question the way the economy is operating, or whether it is generating these problems; it focuses directly on individual responsibility and self-help. Apart from compulsion in participation, the role of the State is minimal.

Model 3: Collective Insurance

As the individual insurance model was tested during the inter-war period and its limitations became evident, two other models of welfare developed. The first of these was the principle of collective insurance. This finally abandoned the old individualist base and openly acknowledged the corporate responsibility of people towards one another in meeting these needs. All contribute on a flat rate or on the basis of their ability to contribute to the care of all who need it. This approach involved a change in the time framework for welfare.

152

Instead of building up contributions to meet future needs and benefits from an accumulated fund, the contributions of the community would go to meet current needs. Because the historical contract approach was no longer present, this led to two further changes. First, the benefits could be changed to meet the circumstances and needs of the moment. (This has tended to happen anyway, because the Great Depression and the Second World War had created such unstable conditions.) Second, this approach required the ability of the wider community to meet these welfare responsibilities to be addressed.

Collective insurance was of course embodied in the Beveridge Report, which was strongly tied to the commitment to *Full Employment in a Free Society*, i.e. a determined attack on unemployment, which Beveridge formulated largely in the terms of Keynes.[4] The system was egalitarian in that it provided flat-rate benefits for all citizens, and it retained an insurance base. Entitlement was by right on the basis of contributions. Beveridge believed that tax financing was more likely to bring an extension of means-tested benefits (on the basis of Model 1). This model introduced a new political dimension to the provision of welfare, for it became the responsibility of each generation to decide what the scale of its contributions and benefits should be. Essentially this was a moral and relational choice. What priority did the contributors give to meeting the needs of those receiving benefits? After the war there was a strong sense of collective responsibility, but this has tended to weaken in succeeding decades.

This model is under attack from a number of directions. First, with the retreat from a full employment commitment, the ability of the economy to meet the benefits is suspect, especially with an increasing number of dependants; Social Security spending has expanded to 30 per cent of all government expenditure, and imposes stress on other departments to cut their budgets. Second, the egalitarian flat-rate benefit approach has been challenged by those who see graduated contributions and graduated benefits as fairer. Third, the scale of the provision of welfare has been criticized by those who see it as expanding dependence and imposing strain on the industrial base.

153

Model 4: State Socialist Rights

This view developed alongside the previous one. For example, Lloyd George introduced pensions as a State-funded right in 1909. (As this example shows, the view was not only held by Socialists.) The nub of this position was a new vision of the role of the State which developed mainly within early socialism. One of the sources of this approach was the German Statist tradition which many of the early Fabian Socialists looked to as a model of the way a socialist State could develop. It emphasized the State as the focal institution of the nation, the basis for national progress and self-fulfilment. Although Bismarck's policies were paternalist, his example was important in showing what a more positive, directive policy for the State could mean. The later example of Leninist Russia gave a more triumphalist note to this faith. The socialist ethos saw the State as providing benefits by right to all citizens who came within the categories of national provision. The benefits were no longer linked to contributions, but resulted from citizenship.

This, of course, raises the issue of what comes within the category of a right of citizenship. With the creation of the National Health Service all health provisions were moved into this category, including dental and optical treatment, school milk, orange juice and prescriptions. Partly because (it was felt) this led to extravagant use of resources and also to raise revenue, this right was gradually compromised, and it is now often modified by appeal to Models 1 or 2. In education the right is still quite fully intact at primary, secondary and tertiary levels. Clearly, there is no systematic pattern of defining what these rights are.

We finally note the freedom which this model gives from any contributory base. Since the funds are raised through general taxation, the rights are not tied to contributions. This, of course, creates the possibility of an expansion in welfare expenditure without any firm accounting base from which to evaluate it, a charge sometimes made against this approach.

The Mosaic Model

The four previous positions will be readily recognized by most people, but there is also another, rather more shadowy one which focuses on relational justice. Models 1 and 2

154

assume that the economy functions automatically in a benevolent way. The collective insurance model relies on a pattern of full employment and the socialist one puts its faith in the efficacy of the State. But none of these approaches actually addresses the issue of why needs and dependence emerge in the wider economy. This model faces this problem more directly.

The previous positions contain echoes of some biblical themes, but when we consider the Mosaic Law, an embryonic statement of God's purposes for a coherent society, another major theme emerges. The prescriptions are no less committed to independence. Indeed, what we would regard as normal employee status was in the Mosaic framework regarded as a declension from economic independence. The hired servant was seen as needing help to fuller independence. Yet independence was not seen as a mechanical and automatic process, but as something which the community works at through its structures and long-term commitment to fairness and to love of one's neighbour. Time and again the refrain comes through: 'If one of your countrymen becomes poor'. At the first stage he might sell property, but the property is to be redeemed. At the second stage he might be unable to support himself, so you must help him as you would a temporary resident. Charge him no interest on what you lend him. At the third stage he might have nothing to sell but his labour. Treat him as a hired worker. The process of impoverishment happened and people were to be helped at each stage to reachieve independence. It was the normal response of neighbourly love and respect, and necessary so that people could walk with their 'heads held high' and 'not look down on their neighbour' (Leviticus 26).

But the approach was not simply remedial, even in this sense; it also contained a structural dynamic. The emphasis was on relational justice and the redistribution of resources to those who had become temporarily dependent. The cancellation of debt, the jubilee reversion of land, the provisions for the hired servant, the usury laws and the distribution of land in Canaan all tended to this result—'that there should be no poor among you'. Relational justice also meant that one group of people in the community should not accumulate, add field to field, at the expense of their fellows.[5]

When the point is made it is obvious. It is going the second mile. The first mile is the provision for the dependent, and that is the aim of the earlier models, but to stop there is to make the problem a permanent one. The second mile is to redistribute resources so that the dependent can become independent. Only that, in the end, will solve the problem. Now of course those whose resources are likely to be redistributed find it very difficult to face this argument. Counter-arguments spring up from all directions. The dependants will waste resources; they do not deserve them; they do not have the skills to use them; they are none of our concern; the power will go to their heads; we must have incentives; we have got to concentrate on the wealth creators; and it will all go on beer and videos. But in the end we have to admit that the poor will remain poor unless they are given the resources to change their situation.

There is another sticking point here which is rooted in the naturalistic exchange paradigm. Everything must be exchange; this is the basis of efficiency and all economic progress. So goes the orthodoxy. But it is not true. We have already noted that 40 per cent or more of the economy is based on gift. We all live in debt to the wealth and resources of previous generations passed on to us (in many different forms), which we have done nothing to earn. And we must recognize our fundamental dependence on God's providence for us, the gift each day of our daily bread and much more Giving, far from being peripheral, is actually the foundation of our economic life. Although the naturalistic paradigm sees the second mile as treason, it is actually sound and well-based policy.

With these five models in place, many aspects of the operation of the Welfare State come into focus. For example, the poverty trap is a problem which can be easily located with Model 1. Crossing the boundary from 'dependence' to 'self-help' is a tough jump financially. But the interaction of the five models also explains the anomalies which occur on the ground. Are pensions going to be seen in terms of Model 1, 2, 3 or 4? All versions are at present on offer. Is the health service going to be a citizen right, a form of collective insurance or a matter of individual insurance? If the latter, is it best done privately backed up by a residual service for those who are not independent enough to provide for their own insurance? Should we let the United States model seep across the Atlantic? Is unemployment pay to be seen as a residual provision for the dependent, or as collective insurance, possibly with graduated contributions and benefits? Policy has changed on this issue also. Clearly, in all the discussion of the Welfare State, the issue of *which* Welfare State needs to be addressed.

Organizational Subversion

Although the ideologies of the Welfare State constitute one level of problem, other ones arise from its institutional operation. For the people who have actually run the organizations have not been the ideology-forming politicians, but groups of middle-class civil servants and other professionals. Their emphasis, despite their best intentions, has often worked against the aims of the models we have considered above. For example, Models 1 and 2 explicitly, and the others implicitly, put great weight on self-help and independence. However, the bureaucracy in charge of housing provision since 1945 has exercised rigid paternalist control. They designed the houses, the neighbourhood and the community. They decorated the houses, maintained them, required them to retain a rented status, and by isolating council houses from areas of middle-class housing, created the largest physical influence on the class structure in Britain. The most outrageous forms of this attitude are evidenced in the housing blocks and tenement units which are currently being torn down in so many big cities. This housing provision grew up within a socialist vision of citizen rights, but has been fundamentally divisive, and the reason is largely to be found in the middle-class attitudes of control held by the local government officers administering the programme.

Sometimes the effect has been even more dramatic. Why is the National Health Service seemingly in decline? Has there been a grass-roots revolution in favour of private health care? On the whole, no. On the contrary, there has been an abiding gratitude for NHS provisions among the population generally. One explanation for current problems is that the Health Service has been largely subverted by its senior professionals. Consultants, by maintaining their select and inaccessible status, have generated delays and queueing within the service, and, in order to open up the more lucrative private practice available to them because of their excellent public training, have viewed with equanimity shortcomings in the public provision. It is quite clear from the statements made by the Conservatives and other parties during the mid 1980s that there is no political opposition to the National Health Service. It seems therefore that the opposition has come from within, largely from the greed and status-maintenance of some consultants. As much of the pressure for abortions came from private doctors making large incomes from them, so the pressure for change in the National Health Service has at the very least been happily accepted by those seeking to open up private practice.

This example underlines a repeated pattern in the Welfare State, namely, the ability of the middle classes to make sure that it operates to their advantage. This is evident in housing provision, where on the one hand council house rents are determined by strict market criteria, but on the other hand private owners receive vast subsidies. These occur through the tax relief on mortgage payments and tax advantages given to building societies. One of these is a process whereby building societies are allowed to deduct tax on behalf of the Inland Revenue at a composite rate, whether the investor pays tax at a zero or a very high rate. This effectively means that the poor investor subsidizes the rich by providing them with tax rebates. The effect of these provisions, especially the tax relief on mortgage payments, has been vastly to subsidize the owner-occupier, especially the ones with very high incomes. This in turn has helped to create a boom at the top end of the housing market, creating massive capital gains for the rich and making the rehabilitation of poorer housing less attractive. Again, we see a market which is heavily structured to favour the well-off.[6] In another area we see the grants to middle-class university students well protected, while inner-city education faces a crisis as the metropolitan areas are abolished and central subsidies are cut. When there are twice as many with degrees proportionally in the south-east as in the north, this has regional consequences as well.[7] The way the system works tends repeatedly to favour the middle classes, who supposedly do not need so much help from the Welfare State.

This whole area of problems can be simplified by saying that there is a conflict between the Welfare State administrative bureaucracy, which tends to favour the middle classes and maintain control, and actually getting resources to those who need them most. Third World Aid agencies sometimes evaluate their activities on the basis of the proportion of their donations which reach the poor for whom they are intended rather than being swallowed up in administration and other costs. Many domestic programmes would score very badly on this criterion, as the Conservatives, using Model 1, began to acknowledge in the mid 1980s. Fortunately, there is a decisive answer to this problem; the transfer of money is swift and efficient. It needs to be substantial, but with careful planning one decision per year per family is capable of solving many of the problems of people and families who are poor. Certainly, it is one of the most effective ways still open to the government to shrink the central welfare bureaucracy, since most decisions of this kind are already taken by the Inland Revenue. Why this avenue of efficiency has not been pursued needs explaining. Sadly, the rich are so opposed to this simple process that they are prepared to create more expensive bureaucratic structures which preserve the middle-class values of maintained privilege and giving nothing away.

The Welfare State and Local Authorities

Another set of problems arises from the definition of local government and its relationship with central government and the Welfare State. The underlying conception of local government is of a variety of local services which are provided as of right to those who pay their rates. In addition central government can require local authorities to provide certain services which are bound up with the welfare of local citizens, but they must also provide the resources necessary for those services. This conception of welfare thus remains a peculiarly centralist one alongside the local government system. This is one of the main reasons why the pattern of provision of services at local level has remained so piecemeal and incoherently organized.

Nevertheless, local authorities are necessarily locked into some fundamental issues which touch on the overall questions of welfare. One was the question of the relation of inner cities and urban areas to their hinterland. This issue was first highlighted when New York went bankrupt in 1974. Modern cities develop a vast suburban and extra-urban territory which depends on and uses the central areas, creating all kinds of costs in terms of violence, environment, servicing and withdrawal which these areas find it difficult to bear, especially if they carry a poor and left-behind residential population. City planners and borough councils have fought against this pattern for decades and redeveloped inner city areas, but in recent years the centrifugal forces seemed to have gained the ascendancy. The abolition of the Greater London Council and the metropolitan councils was partly a move for suburban autonomy. Whatever the details of the ratecapping saga, it works out as a process whereby inner-city spending is pared by the suburban potato peeler.

The rating system also contains its own vicious circle. Roughly half of rate income comes from domestic units and half from factories, offices and shops. Prosperous areas attract and hold families, and especially businesses, which provide a high rateable yield for the area. At the same time these areas have relatively lower potential expenditures—for example, with more cars the costs of local authority transport will be lower. As a result these areas can reduce the rate charged to businesses which therefore move to these areas. Obviously the Rate Support Grant does include compensatory elements, but the overall impact is against the depressed urban area and allows the shire counties to congratulate themselves on their thrift. The Uniform Business Rate (UBR) and the Community Tax proposed in 1986 are attempts at reform; however, the latter is unlikely to redress this problem but rather make it worse.[8] What needs to be considered is whether the distribution of rateable income should automatically coincide with the area in which it is collected. In view of all the regional transfers considered in earlier chapters, there is a need for local authorities to be part of regional policy in a much more fundamental way than is presently the case through the Rate Support Grant. Between 1976 and 1983 not only were the rates of unemployment twice as high in the worst as the best areas, but the rates of increase were twice as high. As *Faith in the City* made clear, government regional policy is hardly redressing the loss of income of inner cities through ratecapping.[9] The distribution of funds through local authority finance needs to be viewed more strategically as a way of radically redressing this impoverishment.

Reform of the Welfare State

When we consider all these factors, the trend has been to submerge the Mosaic distributive justice model. Before the First World War, Lloyd George succeeded in making wealth taxes a substantial part of his revenue through death duty and other taxes. These have now dwindled to a trifling amount, so that little real redistribution of wealth takes place. The same is largely true of income. Lowering of the higher rates by the Conservatives and legitimate forms of tax avoidance mean that there is relatively little redistribution of income, especially when the middle-class uptake of benefits is taken into account. Regional policy has dwindled. And, as we saw in the earlier chapters of this book, banks, business, families and professional organizations are drawing resources from the poor and the unemployed. When we also take into account the power of the middle-class public-sector bureaucracy, it is clear that the economically weak have everything against them.

Yet the Conservative review of the Welfare State set itself narrow terms. It failed to take into account the full weakness of those who should be the primary target of its attentions, and it has largely ignored the concentrations of wealth and income which its policies have helped to create. These terms of reference will not work. Especially, they will not work for the unemployed, except to leave them in the *status quo* situation which is defined by Model 1. A different approach is needed, which goes for the roots of the problem, and it seems evident that it must be constructed around Model 5.

This vision of reform might lead in different directions. Consider one possibility. A progressive wealth tax is needed to modify the massive accumulations of private wealth which are now occurring, and causing rich people to look down on their neighbours; but should that tax simply get lost within the Exchequer? An alternative would be to redistribute it, say £5,000 per person, at the age of twenty-one. The movement of resources to the young, independently of their personal circumstances, would be a major structural change helping to meet the lack of resources they presently experience. In another area the recognition might grow that one of the best ways of getting resources into areas of high unemployment is to increase unemployment pay; it is superb targeting. Yet the trend has been to decrease it. A consolidated tax-benefit system would help create a redistributive system which is not rule-bound and administratively dominated. It could happen quickly, if we were committed to constructive redistribution. The possibilities are there, if the relational concern is given expression in public policy. As God, through Moses, clearly stated, if we intend there to be no poor in the land, the policies are to hand (Deut. 15).

Notes

1. Green Paper on the Welfare State (DHSS, June 1985).
2. For a neat summary of this position see P. Barker (ed.), *Founders of the Welfare State* (Heinemann 1984), pp. 8 – 16.
3. K. G. Banting, *Poverty, Politics and Policy* (Macmillan 1979), pp. 66 – 108.
4. The link between the Beveridge Report (HMSO 1942) and *Full Employment in a Free Society* (Allen and Unwin 1944) is unavoidable; they are an integral policy. See B. Seebohm Rowntree and G. R. Lavers, *Poverty and the Welfare State* (Longmans Green 1951) for a positive contemporary evaluation of the policies.
5. See A. Storkey, *A Christian Social Perspective* (IVP 1979), pp. 335 – 78.
6. See B. Badcock, *Unfairly Structured Cities* (Basil Blackwell 1984), pp. 169 – 288, for a good look at the distributive aspects of housing markets.
7. *Regional Trends* no. 20 (HMSO 1985), p. 93.
8. CBI, *Growth and Jobs* (1986), p. 15. Green Paper on Rates (Dept of Environment 1986).
9. Archbishop of Canterbury's Commission, *Faith in the City* (CIO 1985).

11:   The European Community and Retreat from the World

The European Community

After a long and unsteady courtship, Britain became part of the European Community. The debate at the time tended to focus on the minutiae of a possible profit-and-loss account, on how much the ring would cost; the reality was a far deeper choice, not only politically, but also economically. Joining the Community meant entering a free trade zone where the dynamics of bigger markets were combined with an intense form of economic nationalism. Those who were not geared up to taking advantage of the larger markets would suffer, but they would do so within a certain economic ethos which needs examining very carefully.

The ethos of the Community has developed over a long period in mainland Europe. It goes back to the Zollverein and the process of forming the German nation, and is profoundly different from the Anglo-Saxon naturalistic tradition. It begins with the idea of a protected market. There is freedom of trade within the area where the group or national interest will prevail, but external constraints on trade serve to protect the producers, who are seen as being essential to national well-being. Traditionally the groups in need of protection are the farmers—going back to the Junkers of Prussia—and the major industrialists. Various forms of political ideology— National Socialism, Gaullism, Christian Democracy and Social Democracy—have accommodated themselves to this basic framework. With varying emphases, so have the member nations of the Community.

Let us focus again on the philosophy which underlies this ethos. It involves, at root, trust in the major producers as the guardians of national prosperity. They provide employment, national security and generate wealth, and are the focus of economic policy. The State enters into a tacit agreement to support and protect these producers nationally, or within the

European Community. This corporate philosophy, hammered out as Europe was threatened by American grain and British industrial domination in the nineteenth century remains the conception within which most European politicians automatically think.

What are its results, and how particularly does it affect employment? Giving priority to the producers works as a strategy provided there is demand-side buoyancy. Then the firms are able to expand securely and to provide the employment needed. During the 1950s and 1960s the emergence of the Community led to a buoyant market and the absence of an unemployment problem. The situation is different now — depressed markets leave European countries with no overall unemployment strategy other than that of protecting major companies through trade protection (e.g. the steel industry), or covert subsidies. The policy here is in contrast to the prevailing profit-only criterion of the Conservative governments. The State corporatist policies of Europe led to an understanding that the governments will provide the context and support for the continued viability of these companies. It was inconceivable that the French government would have treated their car companies as BMC was handled by the British; Renault and Citroën are seen as fundamental national assets which command basic government support. But apart from this limited strategy the European Community is bankrupt of policies on employment.

The reason is not far to seek. The *raison d'être* of the Community has been the creation of a secure, protected market. That market is now full of ageing, consumer-goods-saturated people who do not and will not provide the demand dynamism needed by the existing coporate protectionist policy. Its own move for security has guaranteed it a stagnant market. The relationship of Europe to the rest of the world's markets is interesting. It competes with Japan, but primarily for European markets. Competition with the United States will be more limited as that country's soft trade position is finally exposed with the fluctuations in the price of oil. Trade with the rest of the world is limited by the ability of those areas to pay, and by the fact that Eurotechnology is decidedly upmarket and out of touch with the needs of much of the world's population. The corporatist support of the producer tends to lead to overproduction and dumping on some world markets. Indeed, the dumping of European grain in Africa did little to help food producers to make headway in the period before the famine. There is nothing in European strategy and policy which works towards an expansion in world trade and a generation of jobs for overseas consumption, a fact that has been obscured by the expansionist policy of the United States government in the mid 1980s. Europe is locked into her own stagnant affluence. Thus the underlying direction of European corporatist philosophy is on course for more serious world trade depression and unemployment than is already here.

Of course, there are some areas of expansion, like arms sales. Indeed, in the case of the Anglo-Argentinian war, Europe almost succeeded in equipping Argentina to defeat a European member state. This raises the issue of whether the dynamic created by European selling is not, along with Third World demand, partly responsible for many world tension points. Certainly, if there were a widespread outbreak of peace, for which we pray, it would cause even deeper depression, in Europe and Britain especially, where the commercialization of armaments manufacture has proceeded apace.[1] Both in terms of armaments and luxury items, it is amazing how much of what the Third World does not need Europe has been able to sell to them.

Thus Europe sails into the doldrums of maldistribution and surfeit, while the Third World has the dynamic of population growth and change which could radically change the parameters of the world economy.

National Corporatism
Corporatism first came to prominence in the 1930s, where an alliance of major corporations with Fascist governments was seen as a new pattern for totalitarianism. In one sense now it is far less sinister. In another it is more fully developed. For multinational companies have now slipped their national boundaries. They no longer export from a base, but move capital, technology, labour requirements and profits at their discretion. At the same time there is, without the Fascist content, widespread collusion between national governments and these corporations. Because they provide jobs, tax revenue

and investment the corporations are able to claim they are acting in the national interest and to claim the loyalty of the government, whether in Europe, Japan or the United States.[2]

Occasionally a fast-growth area occurs where new multi-nationals can and do spring up, but mainly they are engaged in defending well-established market positions in mining, oil, automobiles, chemicals, telecommunications, engineering, leisure industries, retailing, food, aircraft or transport. The defence of these positions is complex. It involves maintaining dominance in technology, sales, productive efficiency, access to raw materials and managerial expertise. But the rewards are very great. Once this kind of dominance is obtained, it becomes more and more difficult to shake. There is little likelihood that ITT, General Foods, ICI or Shell will be tumbled from their market position in the foreseeable future by young upstarts. It would require probably billions of pounds of investment before revenue began to flow, with the knowledge that in the end one of the companies would be pushed out of the market by a price war. These entrenched positions are not simply established in terms of the market monopoly, but in terms of sites, expertise, relations with government, grants/aid, public contracts and so on. They become bedded down in the economy and social structure.

The challenge to the position of these companies thus comes from abroad. It is at this point that the relationship between multinationals and their national government becomes especially important. National self-interest requires that both work together; which they do. Government constraints, tariffs, bilateral trade agreements, overseas contracts are all supported by the national government, whose success is closely related to the success of its multinationals. Generally this results in a protectionist domestic policy on the one hand, and an empire-building policy overseas. Japan has pursued this policy most successfully, but has been closely followed by Europe.

What is the effect of this policy on employment? First of all, countries which ignore this corporatist policy and operate on a *laissez-faire* pattern, suffer because their corporations lack the power base of the national governments. This undoubtedly happened with Britain during the first decade of membership of the Community. But the longer-term effects are more subtle. The institutional pressures on these companies are to secure home markets, reduce labour costs and increase efficiency, and to plough back all available surpluses into research and development which will allow the company another decade down the line to deliver a major knock-out blow to its chief competitors. Whether in drugs, chemicals, car manufacture, electrical engineering, aircraft or whatever, the open-ended commitment is to research which will deliver the knock-out blow. This high-technology research is capital-intensive. Therefore the net effect is to put labour costs under the firmest criterion of efficiency, while high-technology capital research costs are treated with cheerful abandon.

The most noticeable aspect of this policy is found in the export of labour to low-income territories, whether in southern Europe or in Third World countries. Especially important is the increasing use of free trade areas which is effectively allowing multinationals to escape national boundaries and to exploit the cheapest world labour. Western multinationals are now doing this on a massive scale, which is often not reflected in trade terms, for although the companies are buying in Third World labour they are re-exporting the products of that labour to the Third World or other developed countries. Thus the multinationals are bypassing domestic labour and enjoying the reduced collective power which the unions have as a result of this policy. The multinationals thus have, unless policy changes, a serious depressive effect on employment.

The question this should raise, although it is rarely discussed, is of the fairness of multinational companies moving capital around the world for corporate reasons. Let us express the issue in personal terms. Workers in the west Midlands have worked for most of their lives contributing to the development of a major company, only to find that, on the grounds of 'its' strategic use of capital, it has shipped off the jobs that should be available to their children to Spain or beyond. It seems evident that the workers who have helped to create this capital and market position should have a say in its disposal. Capitalists are often narrow in their concerns and unaware of the damage being done in other people's lives.

The Newly Industrialized Countries

This raises the issue not just in terms of the multinationals, but also in coming to terms with the Newly Industrialized Countries (NICs) which they have spawned. In the early 1960s these countries decided to open themselves to overseas capital and technology and break away from restrictive barriers. Their cheap labour would allow them to penetrate the industrialized markets of the world. The example of Japan was the prototype; Hong Kong followed; Singapore, Mexico, Taiwan, South Korea, Brazil, Spain, Greece, Yugoslavia, Algeria and other countries have moved into this role. They constitute the most dynamic element in the world economy at present; in 1985 Brazil was the fastest-growing national economy. Companies who could transfer production to these economies made massive profits and the countries themselves experienced growth in employment, overseas earnings, per capita income and credit worthiness. It was in these countries that debt was looked at most beneficently.

The obvious consequence was that jobs disappeared in Europe. Clothing, shipbuilding, textiles, electronics, toys, sports goods and shoes all tend to be manufactured in these countries. Air transport now moves many of these goods easily and cheaply, components can be flown over, and the parent company's domestic task is little more than orchestration. There is much injustice in this situation. Workers are treated as production fodder. Unionism is harshly eliminated. It feeds off racialism and other forms of exploitation, and it is fundamentally unfair to workers in Britain and elsewhere who have built up these resources and are then simply discarded. But our concern at present is not to discuss these, but the response of the European Community to this situation. Millions of jobs fly out of Europe as the planeloads of cheap goods fly into our airports. What is the policy?

Basically, there is no policy. The multinationals often already have access to European markets because they live here: imports occur within company accounts. Also, Japanese and American companies can easily afford to pay tariffs and undercut European goods, because of the large margins. It is a classic case of comparative advantage: capital, technology and raw material are relatively mobile, but labour is not; so production moves to the cheap labour. The European response is to hide behind a tariff wall and hope the problem will go away. They also hope that their multinational companies will be dynamic enough in the NICs to create wealth which will lead to more jobs. This, however, is whistling in the wind. The United States and Japan are more dynamic, and when production can be exported, wealth is dissociated from jobs.

Broadly speaking, there are only three long-term responses to this situation. The first is to rely on capitalism, a process whereby the West competitively fights for control of an expanding world capitalist economy. In exchange for cheap imports and raw materials it offers just capital. This option does not seem viable, partly because it is not enough to offer, and partly because it requires control and power, often military, which is dangerous in order to retain high levels of return to the exported capital. Its motivation is a pattern of self-serving and indulgence which is degenerate.[3] The second option is to retreat behind heavy protectionism which will allow a range of productive but expensive occupations to flourish. This pattern is present in European farming and industry at present on a scale few of us have faced. It involves a high valuation of work, but in the end is a long-term retreat. The third option is the most important. It involves asking what the NICs and the developing countries need, and setting out to provide responsive trade. Here the challenge is great, especially because Europeans have moved away from these needs in their patterns of production; they are upmarket almost to the extent of being out of sight. Facing this challenge is crucial to the jobs of millions of people in Europe, and we shall consider it again later in the chapter.

The Internationalization of Capital
Another part of this picture is the emergence of an international *laissez-faire* capital market. Indeed, as we saw in relation to the United States in the mid 1980s, it is possible for the international capital market completely to dominate contrary trends in trade in establishing exchange rates. This is partly the result of electronically-moved money and the growth of international banking, but it is also the result of floating exchange rates and a growth in financial institutions whose concern is to maximize returns on financial

assets. This has led to a massive change in the pattern of international liquidity.[4] What previously was done through government reserves and international agencies such as the IMF is now carried out through private banking debt and the Eurocurrency market. This change has happened in little more than a decade, and yet is a totally new institutional pattern. In 1984/5 the international capital market grew by about 20 per cent, with many new forms of credit. The fluctuations in this market are substantial enough to make the *market* use of the capital more important than its longer-term productivity. The result is to remove capital from a whole range of productive possibilities and to create an international separation between finance and productive capital. The really big returns are to be made through the increasingly volatile exchange and equity markets, and not through long-term productive investment. Increasingly, companies are buying into a high-risk situation, especially with the problems of Third World debt and the United States deficit, which dominates their productive decisions.

The significance of this institutional change needs to be fully savoured. After the Second World War the international community at Bretton Woods was concerned to establish supranational agencies which would have as their aim the stabilization of trade and capital movements. Now, largely through the influence of the United States (and the City of London) this responsibility has been 'privatized' into a *laissez-faire* system of international capital. This raises the question of what these private institutions will do in situations where their own and their national interest do not coincide with longer-term stability. Crucial is the United States trade deficit, currently at $150 billion, and its low savings ratio of 2 per cent. This country is becoming the world's biggest debtor nation (with substantial loans to other shaky debtors like Brazil and Mexico).[5] The controlled fall of the dollar in 1985 opened up the question of what would happen when all the liquidity sloshing around the world in dollar holdings began looking for somewhere else to go. Even substantial falls in the dollar cannot remedy the United States trade deficit, and countries which depend on exports to the States may suddenly see their revenue fall drastically. The spurious structure of the international financial markets will became evident, perhaps with the collapse of major currencies and banks. Whatever the actual process of disruption, the long-term impact of this instability on unemployment will be serious, and it arises out of the unreality which we have been examining.

It would be easy in the face of this crisis in international capital to try to focus on grand solutions, and, indeed, non-privatized ones are needed, but the underlying reality is the way these institutions have been worshipping pure finance and the maximum rate of return in a context which has been becoming more and more unstable and egocentric in its decision-making. High real 'rates of return' are generated more by good work and sound co-operation in the use of resources than by some intrinsic quality of finance, and the bankruptcy of the ideology of the financial empires is now becoming evident. The problem arises because these institutions are not able to invest in ways which provide jobs and meet people's needs; they are merely experts in shunting funds around various financial ports to maximize return in accounting terms. When such institutions need to maximize accounting gain, ways are found of providing that accounting gain. This leads to inflationary and unreal markets which have lost touch with the real productive base of the economies concerned. It is therefore the whole ethos of these institutions which needs to be challenged if this problem is not to become more chronic. Even in large-scale capital markets we need to love our neighbours as ourselves.

World Markets
In the 1960s Britain faced a choice in terms of its long-run trade strategy. On the one hand, there was the possibility of linking up with the countries of the European Community which were affluent, dynamic, growing economies. The link also meant falling in with the producer-protective ethos of the Community and accepting the internal *laissez-faire* doctrines on which it was based. On the other hand, Britain also faced the possibility of opting for a much more amorphous trade orientation which grew out of the links with the old and new Commonwealth. Would it be possible to open up trade with developing nations in a way which would create a viable, long-term trading policy for the nation? This alternative was

171

not taken; Britain went for the rich markets rather than the poor, but within the Community the same issue still faces us as the previously dynamic markets have become stagnant and oversupplied.

At the same time Britain, along with the other countries of the Community, presents a policy to the rest of the world of bloc protectionism. Third World countries face heavy tariffs both for agricultural and manufactured goods, and the transfer of resources away from producers to the tariff-levying bloc is considerable. Whether as suppliers or consumers, the Community is able to use strategies which guarantee most of the time that the terms are favourable. The transition from the oil crisis of the early 1970s to the oil glut of the early 1980s was not just a naturalistic fluctuation, but a carefully articulated response at a number of different levels — financial, technological, macroeconomic and microeconomic — which made sure that the consumers would regain control of the market. On the basis of its market discretion the West has made sure of its wealth, security and protected affluence, or it thinks it has. It pulls down its barns and builds bigger ones and rests on its ability to look after itself.

The meaning of the present situation is best conveyed when we realize that the United States in 1984 received more capital than the whole of the Third World received in non-communist aid. In other words, the rich were lending to the rich on a scale which meant that the poor were effectively being ignored. Yet it is precisely this poor bloc which constitutes the dynamic, population-growing, market-expanding part of the world which should be the focus of the world's work over the coming decades. There is the work, but the policies of the West prevent the West from being able to work for and with these growing economies. Instead we stay shut within our own stagnant enclaves, financially, in terms of trade, by ethos, by the choice of markets and technology, and by our commitment to affluence.

If this situation is to change, and clearly it has deep significance for jobs, then the change in thinking which is required is mindbending. What is needed is the kind of attitude which was represented by Marshall Aid — the identification of need and the generous provision which allowed people to help themselves into productive activity. As the Americans discovered, this kind of economic regeneration opens up markets, exports and jobs far more effectively than carping, scrimping, beggar-my-neighbour attitudes. We need the kind of attitude detailed in the Mosaic Law which saw debt not solely in terms of an asset yielding the maximum return, but as a way of helping people into independence, with the possibility that the debt cannot be returned. Cast your bread upon the waters, for after many days you will find it again. In more direct terms this means that Europe should be prepared to be the larder of Africa. It means that aid should be the biggest growth industry and should be rivalling defence in the government accounts. The time for this kind of giving and help is running out. As Third World countries become more bitter and helpless and the seeds of antagonism grow, each physical bit of help will be worth less and be valued less. The selfish western strategies will be thrown back in the face of the West and the judgement will be more fierce.

Rampant Evil

One of the most sober realities which we face is the ability of people to destroy real wealth. Of course, it pales beside their ability to destroy one another through war, aggression and hatred, yet it is perhaps easier to consider this slighter form of evil. We find that a high proportion of fires result from arson and a desire to claim on insurance. Resources go up in smoke and are lost to us all on a scale which represents thousands of jobs. Yet this is only a small example. The 1984 miners' strike, whoever was responsible, also lost coalfaces and equipment representing thousands of jobs. It is possible to stand in many parts of Britain watching property worth millions of pounds decaying before our eyes or being actively destroyed. Yet even these examples are trivial when compared with the vast waste resulting from the Iran/Iraq conflict, the Lebanese occupation, the Vietnam War, Central American conflicts or the Falklands War. The ability of modern man to destroy wealth on an unprecedented scale cannot be gainsaid.

Yet the focus of much of that waste, especially in the form of armaments, is on economic preservation. Part of the real cost of our egocentric self-interested economics at a personal, institutional and national level is the preservation of wealth through arms accumulation. Economic security on this argument is to be found in military power, and as each side pursues this pattern, the costs rise and bombers, fighters, satellites, tanks and other military hardware sit uselessly around the world, until someone calculates that it is in their interest to attack. The 1983 world military budget was around $660,000,000,000, and there have been sixteen million war-related deaths since 1945.[5] From the outside it is possible to watch the way in which attitudes and policies harden into patterns which lead to conflict. These may result in periods of hyperactivity in some economies, but their effects are inflationary and costly. What we have to fear economically as well as in other ways are the attitudes and self-obsessions which will lead to this outcome. When Mr Carter became President he noted how the dependence of the United States on Middle East oil was a source of likely long-term military conflict. This concern was largely ignored, yet it is precisely this awareness which is needed if other forms of economic waste and devastation are to be avoided. The enemy is economic egocentricity, especially when it is linked to nationalism. And the catastrophes associated with this attitude will now have to be regarded as a normal part of economic life.

Conclusion

The suppositions of this chapter are even more worrying than those of earlier ones. European policy is set in a pattern which precludes a proper response to unemployment. The great corporations have policies of self-survival which often actively undermine domestic employment, and international capital markets are becoming unstable in ways which recall 1929. Protectionism is gaining ground and is already very firmly established in relation to the Third World. Economic catastrophes become yearly more probable. In the face of these possibilities, a very serious increase in unemployment is likely. Here, more forcefully than elsewhere, we face the problems created by a self-interested approach to economics. Ignoring our neighbours is not just wrong, but inevitably the self-interest turns and bites us. We are so close to this situation that the lack of concern is astonishing.

174

Notes

1. Britain supplies 5 per cent and France 10 per cent of the arms transfers throghout the world. See G. Kennedy, *Defense Economics* (Duckworth 1983), p. 221 and *passim* for a good survey.
2. Studies of corporatism includes H. Antonides, *Multinationals and the Peaceable Kingdom* (Clark, Irwin 1978); A. S. Miller, *The Modern Corporatist State* (Conn., The Greenwood Press 1976); L. Hannah, *The Rise of the Corporate Economy* (Johns Hopkins University Press 1976); S. Griffieon, *Facing the New Corporatism* (CLAC 1981).
3. See N. Wolterstorff, *Until Justice and Peace Embrace* (Eerdmans 1983), pp. 22—39 for an interesting discussion of this as a world-system.
4. For an interesting early article see H. G. Grubel, 'The Distribution of Seigniorage from International Liquidity Creation' in R. A. Mundell and A. K. Swoboda (eds.), *Monetary Problems in the International Economy* (University of Chicago Press 1969), pp. 269—82. See also J. Hawley, 'The Internationalization of Capital: Banks, Eurocurrency and the Instability of the World Monetary System' in *The Review of Radical Political Economy*, vol. ii, no. 4 (Winter 1979), pp. 78—90.
5. United States net claims on Brazil and Mexico are about $40 billion. *International Financial Statistics*, vol. 38, no. 10 (IMF, Oct. 1985), p. 123.
6. R. L. Sivard, *World Military and Social Expenditures* (World Priorities 1983), pp. 6, 21.

PART THREE
THE NEW DIRECTION

*This shorter section first draws together some of the policy
implications of the analysis in Part Two to show how the
structural and institutional sources of unemployment can be
tackled. It briefly outlines a whole range of policies which
might address aspects of the problem and work towards the
generation of more paid work.*

*The last chapter looks at some of the deeper aspects of the
problem: how dogma still dominates the debate, how difficult
it is to face our failure, how we personally run away from the
issue, how electoral politics freezes the issue and how the
changes of attitude required to face the issue challenge our
deepest beliefs. For this is ultimately the problem. Unemployment will not be solved by new technical answers, but
requires changed values and commitments and a different
way of understanding our economic relationships. The last
section, therefore, is a restatement of some of the Christian
beliefs out of which the alternative presented here grows.*

12: Policies for Employment

Review

In the previous chapters we have been involved in changing the map of the British economy. The claim has been that the old maps seriously misrepresent what is going on, so seriously that it was not possible to see what should be done about unemployment. They ignored the importance of institutions, their ethos and direction, and the way they are shaping decisions to eliminate jobs. If the institutional analysis of the previous chapters is substantially accurate, it is evident that the old paradigms of monetarist, Keynesian and socialist economics do not give us a reliable enough picture of what is going on, to enable us to respond realistically. By contrast, on the basis of this new map, we can see more accurately where we have gone wrong.

Many detailed points are on the table. A substantial proportion of no-job families remain locked into poverty and worklessness. Financial institutions draw money from depressed areas and fail to channel it into job-creating investment. Companies put a high priority on reducing rather than increasing their workforce. Professionals protect their own positions to the exclusion of others from the workforce. Technology and training are not available to a substantial proportion of citizens, who become marginal workers. The Welfare State perpetuates concentrations of wealth and income which leave the disposable workers without resources. And Europe merely encroaches more on British markets without offering any broader policy for expansion in world trade. In this sense the scenario is no less gloomy than at the start of the book.

Yet we now know we can respond. Markets can be reshaped. Institutions can be restructured in ways which give a strong, positive valuation to employment. Previously the naturalistic, mechanical approaches to the problems came up with manipulative techniques. Now we have a more direct appreciation of our responsibilities. And our responses are

179

not pragmatic, but normative. They involve a careful assessment of the way in which the actions of each of us affect all of us. The myth that we can be short-sightedly self-interested and leave the invisible hand to sort it out is finally dispelled. So too is the single-level, essentialist answer which sees the solution to unemployment in terms of monetary policy, or the reform of the labour market. At all institutional levels a normative response is needed. The possibility and the policies for full employment are there, if our attitudes are right. The heart-throb of these policies is people's assent and commitment to them, in various institutional contexts (not just 'majority' electoral consent). The commitment to the values are part of the policies, and without the commitment, the changes resulting from new policies are likely to be illusory. Thus the old positivist fixation on neutral facts and generalizations finally breaks down as we recognize that our values and priorities shape and reshape the data.

More fundamentally, we recognize that we are accountable to God for our attitude to our neighbour in all these institutional relationships. We must understand with far more care how our actions affect our neighbour. There is still a fundamental choice. Either we seek God's rule of love and right living in our economic lives, so that our neighbour is loved as we love ourselves, with the promise that all these things will be given to us as well. Or we seek first, as we have done, those things, and ignore our neighbour. Christ was quite clear in his teaching of the definitive effects of motives and underlying attitudes on behaviour and human strategy. If the policies are born in double-thinking, their outcome will substantially reflect the mixed origins.

There is also a massive change in the categories of thought in the public arena needed to face this challenge: the abolition of the public/private dichotomy, the refusal of the Left/Right debate, the abolition of the idea that banks and other companies should only be accountable to shareholders, the reawakening of a redistributive direction in the Welfare State and the breaking-open of professional monopolies. Orthodox economics will need to extract itself from the dogmatisms of determinate analysis to face more realistically the areas of discretion which people have and the principles which guide them in those areas. Given the tenacious hold of the orthodox

180

thought patterns, these changes will not be easy, although many of them are ready to crumble already.

The next step is to express the aim of opening up good work in a strategy, a set of policies which will lead to employment. Obviously the government is important, not least because it signals to the nation as a whole what its priorities of justice will be during the life of the government, and it is to this institution which we now turn.

Government Economic Policy

The institutional analysis of the earlier part of this book has deliberately ignored some of the concerns of traditional macroeconomic policy, so that they can be presented in a roundabout way in a new light. It is time now to focus directly on the issue of the government's macroeconomic policy. What should it be?

The suggestion is that it should be expansionary, quite radically so, but in the new direction implied by previous chapters. The monetarist reason for controlling government expenditure—in order to limit inflation—is not compelling. The problem of inflation has as much to do with the institutional development of the financial sector as with the specific immediate size of the Public Sector Borrowing Requirement, which is a variable dependent on the level of activity in the economy and of limited significance as a policy leader. Nevertheless, there are problems of public-sector efficiency in government expenditure, especially in relation to the professions which the Thatcher Government has tackled more directly than previous governments. The conclusion which this seems to suggest is that there is the possibility of a substantial increase in expenditure without greater inflation if the expenditure is firmly channelled directly to those who are with few resources and to rebuilding the infrastructure of rundown areas. The model must be of direct redistributive transfer rather than of feeding into administrative structures. The aim should not be paternalistically to direct how people should be helped, but to get money to the poor, who will develop their own wisdom of use.

Second, taxation needs to change shape. Under the Conservatives there has been an erosion of the earlier distinction between luxuries and necessities. VAT has tended to standardize rates of indirect tax. There is room for wider discretion in VAT rates—0, 5, 10, 15, 20 and 25 per cent. More important is the present substantial exclusion of insurance, banking and other forms of finance from VAT. This leads to a distinct bias in the indirect tax system away from production and the provision of services and towards financial transactions, which needs correcting. Further, there is a need for taxation to be moved to wealth, so that around 20 per cent of taxes would be generated from wealth taxes (including what is presently collected through rates). This would give a long-term redistributive dynamic to the economy. There is also a need for the integration of the tax-benefit system, including family allowance and State pensions, so that its growing inefficiency is countered.

The overriding constraint on the rapid growth of job provision is the high marginal propensity to import resulting from the increase in import penetration during the 1970s and the 1980s. Despite North Sea oil the propensity to import out of extra income is the biggest barrier to domestic expansion. The problem is made more acute by the constraints imposed by EEC membership and by the way national corporatism has led to many European firms gaining almost unassailable hegemony of British markets. The reaction should not be narrowly xenophobic, but should focus on a long-term commitment to a lower exchange rate, action against dumping and discriminatory pricing (including executively imposed duties), good tax terms for research and development, accurate information on goods about the proportion of production costs occurring in Britain and a strong anti-monopoly policy in Europe. In relation to its European neighbours Britain should realize that it cannot meet national corporatism with a flabby *laissez-faire* belief in free enterprise and should fairly protect domestic industry, technology and capital. The international auction of Westland Helicopters at the beginning of 1986 typifies what the trend has been thus far. These policies will not of themselves generate industries committed to import substitution and the generation of new exports, but they will create the right climate and prevent Britain from being the 'soft sell' for the world's goods.

In summary, medium-term policy should therefore concentrate on transfers to the poor, increased expenditure on infrastructure, reorientating taxation to wealth and financial transactions and away from corporate investment and necessities, and on improving the balance of trade. The response is expansionist, but more important is the change of direction away from the south, finance and luxury consumption and towards the north, investment and basic consumption. The underlying argument is that when income and wealth are less equally distributed, a smaller proportion (but more from overseas) is consumed, and depression follows; reversing this trend on the other hand is healthily expansionary. But this medium-term macroeconomic policy is the context for a much deeper structural and institutional programme of reform in which the government's role is primarily legislative.

In the medium term the government may also have to cope with a severe crisis in the financial sector, (hopefully) a decline in world military expenditure, rising non-European commodity prices, stagnation in the United States economy and a recession in United States and South American trade. It will not be a comfortable time.

Longer-term Institutional Reform
These policies are longer-term in the sense that they would take a decade or more to fully bear fruit, but at the same time their effects could be quick and substantial. Clearly, they move outside the old interventionist-noninterventionist debate into a concern with the righteous and just structuring of the nation's institutions. Thus, the role of the State is not control, or decontrol, but the definition of good and fair economic relationships through law. Throughout these reforms the value of good work is allowed fuller expression in a way that opens up fuller paid employment and a more equitable distribution of work. Legal changes do not of themselves produce this result, but the attitudes, decisions, commitment and care expressed within these institutions. These proposals do not constitute a 'political' or even an 'economic' solution to the problem of unemployment but are evidence of a more fundamental change of faith and values which find economic and political expression. Set out below are some suggested policies which grow out of the analysis of the previous chapters.

183

Banks and Financial Institutions

1. Banks and financial institutions in depressed areas should be zoned to limit or prevent the withdrawal of funds to more affluent areas in Britain and overseas. Information about the geographical transmission of funds and detailed categories of investment should be publicly available.
2. Banks should be encouraged to pursue 'employment-rich' policies of investment away from property, dead financial assets and towards local job-rich investment opportunities. This probably means decentralization of investment staff and possibly quotas on the various categories of assets held by banks and financial institutions. They could, for example, be required to provide a quota of venture capital.
3. Just as immigrant communities have set up banks to send funds back home, so new banks should be initiated with local priorities in the use of funds. This will involve limiting the powers of the Big Four to exclude potential competitors and, for example, allowing new banks to use the Post Office Giro for clearing purposes.
4. Following the pattern laid out below, one-third of the members of the Board of Directors of banks should be nominated and elected by customers (*see* Company Boards).
5. The taxation of banks should reflect the seigniorage of the money which they create.
6. The big banks should give a much higher priority to needs rather than simply maximizing rate of return and should carry out social audits to see of what value they are to the community and what the effect of their policies are. These should be made public and evaluated by the customers' representatives.
7. The dominance of the Stock Exchange by old and dead shares should be broken by establishing limited-life shares which more closely approximate the lifetime of the capital input, and which put the emphasis on return over a limited period rather than on fluctuations in capital value.
8. The government should establish standardized, audited patterns of share issue which allow cheap and local

share capital to be raised and break through the rigidity of the centralized market in capital.

9. Financial institutions should be required to give details of all overseas assets purchased, and should pay tax on funds so used to compensate for its non-use within Britain.

10. Higher stamp duty should be charged on insurance and the purchase of existing financial assets, including stocks and shares, to reduce the liquidity of these financial markets, and change the emphasis from speculation in existing assets to the creation of new investment. (More than reversing the change in the 1986 Budget.)

Companies

1. The present bias of company policy towards the interest of the shareholders should be corrected by electing the Boards of quoted companies on the following basis: one-third to be elected by the shareholders, one-third by the workers and one-third by registered consumers of the goods or service. This would give a powerful voice to the consumers whom the company is serving, who are now often patronized especially by near-monopoly companies, and it would also create a situation where control of the assets of the company remains in Britain with the workers and consumers, rather than being subject to the imperatives of international capital. Nationalized companies would have a similar pattern, with one-third of Board members nominated by the government.

2. There should be a full disclosure of information to the Board, and thence to the public, so that the direction of the company can be carefully decided, with full communal awareness of what is happening and might happen.

3. Mergers and takeovers would need to be decided by the Boards of both companies concerned. The possibility of disaggregation of a company could become more normal on the initiatives of workers or consumers.

4. Consumers' representatives on the Board would be responsible for an active product-development policy, the monitoring of the product and the definition of long-term consumer needs.

5. Companies should move strongly to an employment policy which emphasizes four-fifths and three-fifths

185

working rather than full-time and part-time work with appropriate changes in National Insurance contributions and other legal parameters of employment.

6. Company policy should concentrate on the long-term viability of the company in terms of employment, exploring import substitution, exports, expansion, research and more labour-intensive forms of organization. The worker representatives on the Board would be expected to develop this policy.

7. New standard simplified patterns of self-employment and small employment should be established by the government to prevent small firms facing a bureaucratic barrier to employment.

8. The movement of large amounts of capital from depressed areas to more affluent ones or overseas should be subject to decision by the Boards of companies (including employees' representatives), so that if the surplus has been accumulated in the area over a period of time it should not arbitrarily be removed, creating an injustice to the workforce.

9. Companies should not allow capital equipment per worker, scarcity, status and internally generated power to dominate their pay policy which is the responsibility of the whole Board.

10. Larger companies should have a strong regional policy and make sure that northern production units are not supporting southern administrative ones.

11. Mergers and takeovers which merely have as their aim the elimination of competitors and the establishment of secure and profitable monopolies should be ruled out by the Monopolies and Mergers Commission and consumer representatives should be encouraged to work for the disaggregation of existing monopolies.

12. Companies should be taxed in part on the basis of their capital/labour ratios to encourage the labour-intensive employers.

13. Agreements whereby the workforce share risk in their wages and participate in profit-sharing should be encouraged.

14. Ploughing-back of profits and resource development should be encouraged by Boards and by taxation policy.

15. There should be a system of matched government funding to local community contributions to raise capital for companies which go bankrupt in private accounting terms, so that hybrid 'public/private' companies can be re-established.
16. Multinational companies should be brought firmly within the company legislation and required to operate under the supervision of the reconstructed Boards.
17. All goods sold in Britain should be required to state the proportion of the value which is domestically produced.

Professions and Unions

1. The closed shop in professions, quasi-professions and unions should be abolished. Particularly, there should be a clear distinction between qualifications and necessary membership of professional bodies. The judicial function of professional bodies like the BMA and the Bar in relation to professional conduct and competence should be eradicated and the professions become publicly accountable to councils which have 50 per cent customer or client representation.
2. Restrictive practices and patterns of employment in the professions should be removed.
3. Professions and unions should work to see that all tendencies towards a tiered workforce are resisted, especially the preferential treatment of some employees with regard to working conditions, pensions, perks, work location, terms of employment and treatment.
4. Professions and unions should be responsible for job creation through their role in pay negotiations and planning. There should be recognition of how efficient working helps others. Development of policies for job creation—expansion of companies, service expansion, export opportunities, import substitution, preventive medicine, community work, environmental aesthetics, recycling—should receive high priority.
5. There should be a commitment to work import opportunities—language, tourism, construction, education, technology and Third World development.
6. The secure upper-tier career which is feather-bedded will need to be modified through a reduction of differentials

and a modification of pension and other benefits.
7. All employers should be required to offer a certain proportion of person/days experience to schoolchildren.

Families

1. Families should move away from the dual-career pattern to a joint level of paid work of 1.2 to 1.8 jobs and should face the economic consequences of the change. Taxation and other barriers to the change should be removed.
2. More time should be committed to children and other forms of unpaid communal activity, partly to prevent the high costs of vandalism, crime, work failure, low educational achievement and statutory personal supervision. Family allowance could include direct child-responsibility (pre-school) and aged-parent care supplement.
3. Resources should be given to young persons to help them establish themselves in work, marriages and homes (*see* Wealth Tax).
4. It should be recognized that marital and family breakdown is a major source of poverty, overemployment and tension between home and work life. Marriage preparation courses should be introduced in schools, a six-month registration period for all marriages of those under twenty-one, and maintenance payments should be deductible at source.
5. Tax exemption should be granted to families for funds used directly to employ others outside their own family.
6. There should be an emphasis on the redistribution of wealth among families, so that more resources are available to those at present without them (*see* Wealth Tax).
7. Families should take more seriously the job-creating potential of their wealth and discretionary funds to directly and indirectly make work. Giving is an important means of work creation and donations to work-creating charities should be exempted from tax.
8. Families should value the work of British people highly in their purchases, especially when dumping and other forms of price manipulation have affected relative prices. They should have the information for a more careful evaluation of where goods are made.

Education

1. Each person should have access to the same number of years of education by right — say, thirteen years plus two for higher education or vocational training, and all years over that period should be financed by loan.
2. Extra resources of teaching personnel should be allocated to areas of educational deprivation, especially during the first few years of formal education, to prevent a continued pattern of deprivation.
3. Training and job-creation schemes should be expanded and concentrated in areas of employment deprivation.
4. Educational advisers should help people in work, in training and who are unemployed, to decide what they need to learn. The full-time education/full-time work barrier needs rethinking.
5. An education tax should be introduced on workers with certain levels of training and income who are abroad and retain British citizenship.

Political Institutions

1. Information on the geographical transfer of resources within the public sector through central and local government should be made available.
2. Proportional representation should be introduced to help lessen swings of policy and develop greater continuity of policy.
3. A wealth tax should be introduced, with people assessed every ten years and paying progressively up to 3 per cent of their assessed value annually. It could be used as the basis for local government funding, with the revenue collected on the basis of wealth and distributed on a modified population basis (thus allowing regional redistribution). Or it could be used in part for block payments to those reaching adulthood, to give resources where they can be more dynamically used.
4. A consolidated tax and benefit scheme should be set up, incorporating family allowance, unemployment pay, State pensions, etc. All means-tested benefits would be eliminated into the scheme. The income tax component should have a more progressive profile, and an increase in marriage allowance should be matched by a job tax on two or more full-time-job families.

189

5. There should be heavy investment in housing, public building, infrastructure and other forms of capital necessary for efficient and prosperous cities. A deliberate policy of redistribution away from affluent local authorities towards those which are severely depressed, especially urban priority areas, should be followed both in departmental expenditure and through a population basis for distributing wealth tax funds to local authorities.
6. There should be a rigorous policy of distributing public-sector employment equitably by area — doctors, teachers, civil servants, public amenities — with positive discrimination to those areas where unemployment is most serious.
7. Third World aid should be radically increased and backed by an export drive to meet the development needs of those countries.
8. The government should curtail the commercial trade in arms within a framework of intergovernment transactions to encourage a rapid reduction of world arms expenditure.
9. The government should operate a policy of a relatively low exchange rate (to encourage our export base and prevent the Dutch Disease) and aim to maintain exchange rate stability without becoming a full member of the European Monetary System.
10. In all government departments public representatives elected by voluntary agencies and other interested parties should have a monitoring role, the right to receive information and rights of accountability in relation to the ministers and departments. They should present annual reports to their constituency.

The European Community and other International Organizations

1. There should be a continued movement from agricultural subsidy towards a broader conception of employment-generating subsidy based on the levels of income per capita of different areas, not necessarily countries.
2. A sharp reduction in European Community tariffs for Third World countries should be negotiated along with

reductions with other countries accompanied by a float down of exchange rates.

3. A strong policy to prevent national corporatism leading to unfair trade and competition should be developed by the Monopolies and Mergers Commission, the Department of Trade and Industry and the European agencies.
4. There should be a commitment to supporting African food production during the next decade with raw materials and resources.
5. The Community should operate a ratcheted band exchange-rate policy both within the Community and in relation to the rest of the world.
6. Movements of 'hot' money should be regulated and taxed.
7. An extension of IMF borrowing facilities which is linked to the standard of living within the debtor countries should be established.

Dynamic Change
Economists are not good at understanding how longer-term change takes place. They tend to think in terms of an idea which is then implemented, but meanwhile all kinds of other events take place and people prove cussed and refuse to get inside the idea. The official left-wing ideology of change is not much more successful; it sees a policy implemented through a centralized bureaucracy which establishes the new way, but this approach seems always to bury itself in a cottonwool wall of inertia and unwillingness on the part of the general public. Against these two positions is a third which shuns theory and ideas on the one hand and centralized control on the other. It sees free enterprise and unfettered entrepreneurs as the necessary dynamic for change. This alternative seems to make some sense in the United States, a younger, more open and loosely organized country than our own, but less with our tightly woven economic life. It can also lead, it seems, to the dominance of one ideology and set of values, which do not entail great care for the economically weak. Can any dramatic agenda for change work in Britain? Are we a rather aged and traditional society which will always demurely walk behind the changes which would meet our problems?

191

This possibility becomes more acute the longer the divisions between upper- and lower-tier workers, north and south, the wealthy and the impoverished, are allowed to grow. Already reform is far more difficult than it would have been at the beginning of the 1980s. We have especially suffered because the adversarial system of British politics means that only one dimension of policy holds the public imagination at any one time as the debate between left and right. Sadly, the concern with inflation, as defined by the party in power, dominated the political debate for most of the 1980s, with the result that unemployment was treated as a residual concern. Yet, although all kinds of other national economic problems will arise, there is still another more realistic way of seeing change. Its realism is found in the overt recognition it gives to our stewardship of the economy.

The suggested dynamic is different. It locates the initiative in two places which have often had very little emphasis in recent British history. The first is on a set of values which includes a sense of justice and neighbourly fairness. The old orthodoxy which sees the promotion of self-interest as natural and has eliminated the theory of value from economics has also engendered a fairly automatic knee-jerking set of interest-group responses which tend to tie change down within narrow parameters. Yet there are important values and commitments to fairness and care in British culture. Sometimes they break through, as with the BandAid experience, but normally they are contained within the interest-group culture which shapes our institutional life. Perhaps they are not strong enough, but alternatively there may be enough vision beyond immediate self-interest for organizations, not just individuals, to travel in a new direction. This issue is discussed more thoroughly in the next chapter.

But the second dynamic is institutional reform. Hitherto, the 'radical' party of British politics, the Labour Party, has been hindered by its statist ideology from undertaking this kind of reform. Although it is an anti-capitalist party, in seventeen years of government since 1945 it has undertaken scarcely any reform of capitalist institutions, other than nationalization. The *laissez-faire* attitudes of the right, and their comfortable relationship with established and establishment institutions, have resulted in a similar quietism. As a result the British have little conception of institutional reform and oscillate between statist control and individual initiative with a tacit assumption that they have no responsibility for the structure of their institutions; it is externalized as 'the system'. Breaking this pattern would be a great dynamic appropriate to a complex economy where people would like to exercise initiative within fair and careful institutional ground-rules.

This kind of change as set out in the medium and long term strategies above is a far more viable approach than those normally adopted. Yet, although possible, it would be false to suggest that a wave of public opinion and votes could carry it through. The difficulties are not technical ones. They are not created by faults in the arguments of the previous pages, although those are undoubtedly present. They are not caused by the complexity of structural change. They drive back to the issue of our deepest commitments and faith. This must be the focus of our final chapter.

13: Unemployment — An Issue of Faith

The Weight of Dogma

Everyone is aware of the presence of dogma in the present debate about unemployment. Monetarists, Keynesians and socialists are talking across one another and travelling in different directions. There are some who have made it their business to construct compromises between these positions. They are sometimes called 'wet' for their pains, but even these compromises do not offer a real hope of reconciliation and growth; they are stirring oil and water. They also have only a nominal allegiance among the wider public, who are not easily committed to a compromise. So the dogmas, although crumbling, continue to hold sway. But if the analysis of naturalism at the beginning of this book is only partly true, the dogma we see is only the tip of the iceberg. Underneath it are all the preconceptions about the nature of the economy, the inexorable movement of 'the tank', which Keynes found himself fighting in the 1930s. Until these dogmas are out in the open and questioned more directly, the debate about unemployment will continue to have an unreal quality.

Nor can we hope much of the economics profession. The leading economists of the day are still those who were brought up on Samuelson and Lipsey, or perhaps Hayek. They imbibed naturalistic, positivistic, determinate, value-free economics with their mother's milk. Many of them have so much intellectual capital invested in these ways of seeing things, that they cannot easily change. If we have to wait until a generation of economists retire, change will be traffic-jam slow. We need to step outside these received positions more quickly. Perhaps this process has already started at numerous different points.

Somewhere close to the centre of this issue of dogma is the question of self-criticism. If we listen to the kinds of noises which have issued from the economic debate, especially since unemployment has become more acute, the timbre of the sound has been one of blame and criticism — of circumstances,

195

groups, policies and stratagems. But always the criticism stays external and distanced. The problem is never with us, with our ways of understanding things, our lifestyles, our attitudes to others and our priorities. Underneath the discussion the tune being played is still the Enlightenment theme of the goodness of humanity and the ability of unaided reason to sort things out. The hard nut is that there is nothing really wrong with us, and it will not easily crack. The strength of all our egos is inside it. Over two centuries we have built up various rationalizations and excuses to defend ourselves against God's requirements in our economic lives; they may be crumbling, but they will be defended to the end.

Dogma is always related to faith, and the economic dogmas which shape our present responses grow out of a deep commitment to The Economy. Since the days of the great prophet, Adam Smith, we have made ourselves an idol and have bowed down and worshipped it. We have prayed to it and said, 'Save us, you are our god.' We have trained special soothsayers who can tell us what the economy says to us and what it tells us to do, but they have failed us. Perhaps it is time to grow beyond this idolatry into a mature evaluation of what our stewardship of the economy should be. We can replace the idol with our responsibility to God, and recognize that we are accountable when 'it' harms and devalues people's lives. The era of naturalistic and positivistic economics should now be at an end, to be replaced by a more self-critical evaluation of our economic activity and our failings.

Fatalism and Failure

One of the dogmas of naturalistic economics was determinism. Sometimes it was expressed in terms of models with the same number of equations and variables. At other times it was a determinate system which politicians and economists could only observe. Others saw it in terms of market forces which sorted out the way the economy behaved. The power of this view can perhaps now be seen in other terms. It was, rather, a process of enslavement whereby people were brought into bondage by the forces created by naturalism. We have seen how a more realistic view recognizes the area of discretion which decision-makers have. Immediately this moves us outside a fatalistic approach to unemployment.

196

Things can be done and we have the responsibility to do them.

Although we no longer face the situation fatalistically, we still address it with a deep sense of failure—in national, institutional and personal terms. One of the results of this failure is the reduction in discretion which people now have. They cannot find jobs, businesses have closed, funds are not available for public expenditure and couples cannot afford another child. Put bluntly, we have dug ourselves into a hole and will have troubles getting ourselves out. Facing this failure is crucial. Many, whom it has not touched personally, are quite happy to ignore it. Yet if we do not view it fatalistically and do not blame external factors (and with North Sea oil it is difficult to do it with conviction), where does the blame lie? The argument of the previous chapters locates the problem centrally in the way *we* relate to one another economically—through institutions, transactions, transfers and priorities. Our failure has been indifference, exploitation, using one another, disrespect, job failure, antagonism, laziness, lack of service and a desire for instant self-gratification at the expense of others. It is a long, bitter and unflattering record.

But the failure is deeper still. The evidence, or at least the symptoms, are present for all to observe. They are present in the level of alcoholism, in the growth of crime, and especially economic crime, and the assumption which is increasingly made that people are expendable for even the most trivial gain. They are seen in the absurdity of some of the items on which money is spent, and the way in which so many of our purchases harm us. If we take into account overeating, smoking, excessive speed, alcohol abuse, drugs, car dependence and other areas of harmful consumption, it is clear that something like 10—15 per cent of consumption is of 'bads' not 'goods'. We do not know where we are going and do not have the criteria by which to establish our priorities and values. Instead of faith providing criteria for valuation of goods and activities, the latter autonomously provide the basis for faith. It is the crisis of this faith which is being worked out in the symptom of unemployment. The emptiness and failure of economism is beginning to dance before our eyes.

The change in attitude which it demands is best described

197

by the word repentance. At national, institutional and personal levels there is a need for remorse at the way we have lived. There is no technical failure, but only our stubborn wilfulness to do it our way. The story is written in our inner cities, in the lives of the unemployed, in the antagonisms of work, in those who have guaranteed their affluence in a relatively unproductive economy, and in apathy. Facing these realities and our responsibility for them, rather than escaping from them into new palliatives, is firmly on the agenda. Our past policies and attitudes are under judgement, and the only mature response is repentance. Collectively we have been indifferent through our voting, public policies, work patterns and decisions to the situation of the unemployed. Our attitude has been to pass by on the other side and pursue our own greed. The agreed callousness of public policy is something we harden ourselves to pursue – or we repent; there is no other option.

There is also a deep need for forgiveness in economic life. We are surrounded by deep hurts: people who have been discarded or whose lives have been ruined by others; and those who are looked down upon by their neighbours, near or distant. There is aggression and revenge in industry and on the streets. People have been betrayed by unfair employers or unions. The scale of this problem is often hidden, but the abrasive, unco-operative, disorganized pattern of our economic life often simply reflects a mild form of revenge and lack of forgiveness. The Scriptures emphasize the close relationship between repentance, forgiveness and restitution, and that all involve a titanic work of God in human hearts. The need for a restitution of peace through forgiveness is thus one of the greatest economic needs. The absence of it ties us into our past and its destructive patterns.

One of the fruits of this kind of change is the recognition that most of the constraints which we experience are self-imposed. If we acknowledge how wrong we have been, then we also see that the unemployed can be helped. We are a rich economy with little pressure in terms of population growth. We have North Sea oil. A communal response to unemployment is possible, one which is determined and swift.

Me and Unemployment

What is our response? If we are without work, the issue is direct and immediate. It brings into question previous jobs, provision for the family, coping with old age, what to do each day, what other people including our marriage partners and children will think of us and what jobs we could do. There may be other tragedies such as alcoholism, depression, withdrawal, marital breakdown, homelessness and death associated with job loss. Some people have felt compelled to pretend to their families that they are still working months after they have lost their job — going off to 'work' each morning in the public library. Others are able to adjust to the situation with realism and a deepened sense of values. Some people know very few who do have work. Others are lost among the dynamically 'successful'. What hurts is the way in which the jobless are imaged, defined and typed in this situation — other people's judgements.

Is the person without a job a failure? Who says what failure is? (The successful people?) Is success related to economic status? Is a wife to be labelled by her husband's job or lack of it? The personal judgements that hem people in are demeaning and destructive, and like all such judgements they finish by being hypocritical. Wine, racehorses and cruises are responsible, but beer, gambling and holidays in Spain are irresponsible. Making money is laudable, helping people is 'soft'. Enjoying oneself when one is unemployed is taboo. Many of the middle classes claim the automatic right to pass judgements on those who are without work. Prejudice and Pharisaic disapproval rule. If the 'dispensables' are given money, they will use it irresponsibly. All these judgements, some of which lie very close to the feelings of the unemployed, compromise basic standards of personal respect and integrity before God.

Most of us view unemployment from the outside, and we are frightened by it. It is a threat to many of our deepest-held commitments — to affluence, to job status, to our place within the community; and if we do not need to, we refuse to face it in personal terms. We also, as we have seen, construct elaborate ways, such as monetarism, of washing our hands of any responsibility for the situation. 'How difficult things must be in the north. There are jobs about if you accept the right wage. We've got to have a time of belt-tightening.' Many middle-class people do not have the social skills to face anything so outside their daily routine. The barriers of class, area, education, race and age make it impossible for upper-tier workers to meet a young, unemployed West Indian and appreciate his predicament. Television in a cosy home does not jump the gap. The overwhelming response is insulation — personal withdrawal into safety. And then there is the daily pressure of our work, our careers, our social life, the children, or the smugness of our pension.

For many of us the question is the level of our response. Consumption creates jobs and so it is no good just going for the ascetic life. That will not help anybody. Do we therefore leave it to the government? These alternatives miss the point. The point is that we can care and do something in a whole range of family and wider public decisions. It is not easy, but it is possible.

A New Coalition
The old orthodoxies in economic policy are crumbling, but how quickly they will fall is difficult to see. They embody powerful established bodies of thinking and are represented by well-established groups. It would, for example, be easy for older defeated Keynesian groups to reorder and defeat the monetarist domination of the 1980s. Indeed, the Employment Institute formed in 1985 has something of that character. But at the same time many are aware of the inadequacies of the old answers. In the late 1980s the orthodox positions and dominant parties have relatively low levels of support. The old loyalties have dissipated into a much wider agnosticism about policy. The old rhetoric is still present, but the hollowness of the arguments is sensed by a higher proportion of the population. Yet the agnosticism is not particularly healthy either; it hovers, is close to cynicism and can be a way of avoiding decisive action.

This situation is matched politically by the unreality of the present system of government. The British electoral system is fundamentally unrepresentative, and this weakness is especially marked when a two-party system begins to break down. The same pattern occurred in the 1930s with the decline of the Liberals. Now Labour has become the third

200

party in the south, although not in the north, of Britain. The Conservative hegemony of government is spurious and out of tune with the convictions of a high proportion of the electorate. The fulcrum of the electoral debate probably lies with the long-term growth in support for the Alliance parties. Whatever the policies of these parties, their supporters probably include an incredible range of attitudes, principles and policy commitments. The underlying question is whether this group contains the convictions and commitments to shape an attack on unemployment. It is a difficult question, especially in view of the problems of constructing new categories of thinking which carry conviction.

But another change is taking place. Conventionally, the public debate was political. Each party had its allies, be it the unions or business. The scope of the debate was what the party said they could do for us, the electorate. The neat political boundaries were comforting. However, it soon became clear that changes were needed in wider socio-economic life without which they were powerless to effect the improvements which were wanted. Political ideology is no longer enough. The new convictions have begun to take shape. On the one hand, there are the old optimists who trust material progress, human understanding, technology and the goodness of humankind. On the other, there are those who have deep misgivings about the way we live and the optimistic answers. Self-criticism and reform are needed if we are not to murder ourselves with our own pride.

The Churches have an important position in this new wider debate. They are able to show the fallacy of man-centred approaches. The biblical doctrine of sin gives a full personal and structural account of the depths of our failings, and the Scriptures give the normative guidance which leads away from self-interest and indulgence. The fulcrum of the situation is human accountability before God, not our own clever answers. The Churches have also begun to realize the inadequacy of the division between the sacred and the secular, which had allowed them to ignore public events as irrelevant to matters of faith, as *Faith in the City* shows. In the biblical text and in daily life it is clear that public events are God's concern and come within the scope of the Good News. The deeper values of all of us are challenged.

201

A New Paradigm

The previous chapters have developed a paradigm which is Christian in its inspiration. The detailed arguments may be amiss, but the general line of response to unemployment represents a challenge to current orthodoxy. It implies that the old tired assumptions which have their roots in the Enlightenment are dead; they have created irresponsible responses. We have often lived on Christian capital in terms of our practical moral responses, while the theoretical structure has been hedonistic, rationalistic and positivistic. But gradually the humanist idea of autonomy and self-reference has taken over, and the consequences of this commitment have become evident. It is this dominant paradigm which is being challenged. The Christian alternative has been behind the preceding analysis, and it is perhaps worth reiterating in this final section the key principles by which Christians steer in their response to economic issues.

The first is a recognition of the centrality of our relationship with God in economic life. God's blessing, care, providence, creation, requirements and mandates are the context for our economic life. We are stewards of God's creation and dependent on its goodness. This means that economic life cannot be considered in a separate compartment (there is no economic man), but is part of our response to our Creator.

Following from this central truth is a recognition of responsible economics. We really can push 'the tank' over the cliff and recognize our responsibility to God for our work, decisions, for our neighbours and for the direction of our economic life. Especially, we can reclaim our responsibility for unemployment and poverty. As we produced it, by neglect, institutional change and our economic geography, so we can adopt responsibility for its cure. We can take up the harness as stewards of our bit of the creation to see what welfare we can produce. The old fatalism of the onlooker is dead.

Our economic life is also economically guided. There are norms of loving one's neighbour, of fairness, of not stealing or coveting, of giving service, which are basic to healthy, communal, economic life. Peace, justice and respect should characterize the terms of our economic relations. The polarities of free-market economics and socialism are both mistaken, for market relationships are structured by norms,

202

and the norms have a deeper relational significance than those imposed by the State for planning reasons. God has given us guidance on the way we are meant to live, and we should heed it.

And our economic life is fundamentally relational. Economics is not primarily about producing things. There lies the route to obsessions. Seek first God's rule of your lives and God's way of right living and all these things will be given you as well. A maximizing economics which throws all relational problems into the welfare dustbin has missed the point. The norm, 'You shall love your neighbour as yourself', is not an optional afterthought, but is central to the meaning of economic life.

Nor are these relations just interindividual. Just as the law and the prophets addressed the structures of the nation, and just as Paul's letters brimmed with recognition of God's concern for all the structured areas of life, so the meaning of institutions needs to be opened up. Rather than the family being seen as a consumption pit into which the world's goods are poured, it is recognized as a responsible, developing, principled unit. Rather than banks being seen as optimizing units, we recognize that they have a unique structure and faith which are expressed in the policies which they pursue.

A Christian awareness includes facing human sin and injustice, especially those forms which are closest to us. They have structural forms. They are buttressed by self-justification and convincing arguments. We deceive ourselves and the economic truth is not in us. Maximization is often a synonym for selfishness and injustice. Our own compromised lives make us run away from honesty. The economics profession has a problem with sin, not just in the behaviour it examines, but also in its practitioners. They are proud with careers and being right. They are compromised by their lifestyle. They are marked by their lack of concern. The arrogance of much economics raises the issue of whether the foolishness of God is not wiser than the wisdom of economists.

Another of the forms of sin evidenced in economic life is idolatry. Some god or other is made the focus of goals and economic activity. Efficiency, growth, competition, profit, consumption pleasure and technology have become at different times the driving force, the authority before which

203

people must bow. Each of these gods induces its own form of slavery, and most of us know in one way or another our own forms of bondage. The biblical message is that the service of God and Mammon are mutually exclusive, and clearly all these forms of idolatry need to be firmly put into place before God.

Facing these realities is not the end of the Christian message. Throughout it is a deeper hope which holds for both the overemployed and the unemployed. It is best expressed in the words of Christ: 'Come to me, all who are weary and burdened, and I will give you rest. Take my yoke upon you, and learn of me; for I am gentle and humble in heart, and you will find rest for your souls. For my yoke is easy, and my burden is light.' May it be so for all of us.

Introductory Christian Economics Bibliography

Biblical

Dow, G., 'What Place does Work Have in God's Purpose?' (*Anvil*, 1984), pp. 139–53.

Storkey, A., *A Christian Social Perspective* (Leicester, Inter-Varsity Press, 1979), ch. 14.

Vaux, R. De, *Ancient Israel: Its Life and Institutions*. London, Darton, Longman and Todd, 1973.

Wright, C., *Living as the People of God*. Leicester, Inter-Varsity Press, 1983.

Perspectival and Philosophical

Clouse, R., ed., *Wealth and Poverty: Four Christian Views of Economics*. Illinois, Inter-Varsity Press, 1984.

Dooyeweerd, H., *A New Critique of Theoretical Thought*. (Philadelphia, Pres. and Reformed, 1955), 4 vols.

Dooyeweerd, H., *Roots of Western Culture*. Toronto, Wedge, 1979.

Ellul, J., *The Technological Society*. New York, Vintage, 1964.

Ellul, J., *Money and Power*. Illinois, Inter-Varsity Press, 1984.

Goudzwaard, B., *Aid for the Overdeveloped West*. Toronto, Wedge, 1975.

Goudzwaard, B., *Capitalism and Progress*. Michigan, Eerdmans, 1979.

Griffiths, B., *Morality and the Market Place*. London, Hodder & Stoughton, 1982.

Griffiths, B., *The Creation of Wealth*. London, Hodder & Stoughton, 1984.

ICHE, *Justice in the International Economic Order*. Michigan, Calvin College, 1978.

Storkey, A., *A Christian Social Perspective*, chs. 13–14.

Stott, J., *Issues Facing Christians Today*. Basingstoke, Marshalls, 1984.

Vickers, D., *Economics and Man*. Philadelphia, Craig, 1976.

Wogaman, P., *Economics and Ethics*. London, SCM Press, 1986.

Wolterstorff, N., *Until Justice and Peace Embrace*. Michigan, Eerdmans, 1983.

Theoretical

Block, W., *et al.*, eds., *Morality of the Market*. British Columbia, The Fraser Institute, 1982.

Cramp, A., *Notes Towards a Christian Critique of Secular Economic Theory*. Toronto, Institute for Christian Studies, 1975.

Cramp, A., *Economics in Christian Perspective*. Toronto, ICS, 1983 and OCC.

Goudzwaard, B., *Ongeprijsde Schaarste*. The Hague, Van Stockum, 1970.

Graham, F., *et al.*, *Reforming Economics* (Michigan, Calvin College, 1986), 2 vols.

Kee, B., *Prijzen en Produktie*. Amsterdam, VU, 1982.

Wilber, C., and Jameson, K., *An Inquiry into the Poverty of Economics*. Indiana, University of Notre Dame, 1983.

History of Economic Thought

Appleby, J., *Economic Thought and Ideology in Seventeenth Century England*. Princeton, University Press, 1978.

Bieler, A., *La Pensée Économique et Social de Calvin*. Geneva 1959.

Graham, F., *The Constructive Revolutionary: John Calvin and his Socio-Economic Impact*. Atlanta, John Knox Press, 1978.

Baxter, R., *The Christian Directory*.

Ruskin, J., *Unto This Last*. London, George Allen, 1900.

Tawney, R., *Religion and the Rise of Capitalism*. Pelican 1938.

Tawney, R., *The Acquisitive Society*. London, Collins, 1961.

The Churches and Economics

ACUPA, *Faith in the City*. London, Church House Publishing, 1985.

Santa Ana, J. de, *Separation Without Hope?* Geneva, World Council of Churches, 1978.

Preston, R., *Church and Society in the Late Twentieth Century: The Economic and Political Task*. London, SCM Press, 1983.

Sheppard, D., *Bias to the Poor*. London, Hodder & Stoughton, 1983.

Walzer, M., *The Revolution of the Saints*. Massachusetts, Harvard University Press, 1965.

Issue-Related

Griffioen, S., *Facing the New Corporatism*. Toronto, CLAC, 1981.

Moynagh, M., *Making Unemployment Work*. Tring, Lion, 1985.

Mullin, R., *The Wealth of Christians*, Exeter, Paternoster Press, 1983.

Vanderkloet, E., ed., *A Christian Union in Labour's Wasteland*. Toronto, Wedge, 1978.

Index

adversarial relations:
  industrial   43, 103-4;
  voting   44, 192
Africa   173, 191
agriculture   4, 22, 123, 163
aid   172-3
Allen, G. C.   105
arms sales   106, 124-5, 165,
  173, 190
Attlee, Clement   9
autonomy   70, 98, 196

banks: in general   30, 41,
  83-95, 184-5; Bank of
  England   89;
  international   49, 169-71;
  norms of   83-5
Becker, Gary   33n, 147n
behaviourism   68
Beveridge Report   36, 153
Beveridge, William   9, 36, 53,
  56, 149, 153
Bible   71-4, 77, 83-4, 99-100,
  104, 139, 103-4
birthrate   145
Bismarck, Otto von   154
Blaug, Mark   67
blessing   71-2, 131, 137, 202
Brazil   168
British Medical
  Association   118, 120, 187
Brown, George   44, 59
building societies   85-6, 143,
  158
Bullock Report   112
Butler, Rab   9, 37

Calvin, John   84

capital: in general   13, 55,
  169-70; capital/labour
  ratio   54, 121-2, 186;
  capital/output ratio   48;
  export of   113, 165, 168
capitalism, capitalists   13, 22,
  54-8, 98-101, 167, 169
ceteris paribus   24
Chadwick, Edwin   150
change   191-3, 200-4
Christ   71-2, 80-1, 180, 204
Christian economic
  perspective   ix-x, 65-82,
  177, 202-4
Churches   53, 99, 201
Churchill, Winston   12
cities   84, 86-9, 99, 122-6,
  137-8, 145-7, 159-61, 190
City, The   14, 31, 85, 87, 90,
  94, 112, 138, 143, 170
classical economists   6, 37,
  53, 57, 149
command economy   55
Commonwealth   171
community   45, 83-4, 153,
  155, 163, 187
companies: in general   26-7,
  41, 43, 74-5, 91-4, 97-113,
  115-17, 120-5, 141-4,
  164-70, 185-7; Board
  of   111-13, 185-6; company
  discretion   102, 105;
  concentration of
  ownership   108-9;
  multinational   28, 41, 109,
  113, 165-9, 187
Competition and Credit
  Control   89, 138

207

firm *see* company
forgiveness 198
Fowler, Norman 149
free enterprise 22, 110, 163, 191
Friendly Societies 151
Full Employment in a Free Society 36-7, 153

Gaitskell, Hugh 9
General Theory of Employment, Interest and Money 8, 38
Germany 43, 59, 101, 111-12, 154, 163
gift 71, 131-2, 136, 156
God 69-72, 74, 77, 79-81, 100, 128, 155-6, 162, 180, 196, 198-9, 201-4
Gold Standard 12
goods 69, 78-80, 197
Goudzwaard, Bob x, 81n
government: in general 166, 181-3, 189-90; borrowing 17, 40; expenditure 12-13, 17, 39, 41, 49; policy 36, 42, 123-6, 164-5
Graham, Fred x, 84n
Greater London Council 160

Hansen, Alvin 40
Hicks, John 32-3, 37, 40
historicism 57
housing 138, 157-8

ideological justification 8-10, 56
idolatry 56, 62-3, 77, 196, 203-4
imports 44, 88, 108, 139
income: in general 13, 23, 35, 38-41, 46-9, 85; distribution of 107, 141, 146, 183
independence of supply and demand 22-3

individualism 72
Industrial Reorganization Corporation 45
inflation 9, 12, 17, 31, 40, 66, 106, 108, 137-9, 181, 192
information 49-50
institutions: in general 22-3, 31, 40-6, 61, 65-6, 73-5, Part 2 passim, 192; breakdown of 2, 42-6; self-referring 85-9, 97, 104, 126
insurance: collective 152-3; individual 151-2
interest groups 14, 43
interest rates 17, 47, 84, 106
international capitalism 13, 55, 85, 169-71, 174, 185
international liquidity 170-1, 191
investment: definition 46, 143; in general 40, 44, 49, 85-9, 91-4, 107-8, 138, 141-4, 167
invisible hand 70-1, 180
Israelites 74, 115

Japan 43, 88, 104, 120, 164, 166, 168
justice: in general 56-8, 62, 66; in employment 121; relational 154-6; in NICs 168

Keynes, John Maynard 1, 6, 8, 23, 35-8, 53, 56, 67, 140, 153, 195
Keynesianism 1-2, 13-15, 38-51, 85, 126, 139, 179
Kuhn, Thomas 15

Labour Governments 37, 44, 107-8, 126
labour market 12, 19-20, 28, 35-6, 44, 54, 57, 97, 115-29, 132-7, 145-6, 168-9, 187-8

normativity 21, 23-5, 36, 38, 40-2, 50, 62, 83-5, 99-103, 111-13, 180
norms 21, 27, 42, 66, 72-4, 101-2, 104, 131-2, 202
North-South divide 85-9, 124-6, 183

objectivity 6-7, 67-8
oil 4, 31, 172, 182
onlooker stance 70
overdetermination 39

paradigm 5, 12, 15, 24, 38-9, 55, 61, 65, 68, 77, 156, 202-4
planning 44, 59, 61
pluralism 74-5
Pollard, Sidney 107
positional goods 47, 141
positivism 6-7, 50, 62, 180, 195
poverty 71, 74, 84, 86, 145-6, 172
price elasticity: of commodities 25-7; of consumers 25
private sector: in general 18, 45, 50, 62, 110-13; insurance 151
professions: in general 74-5, 115-29, 181, 187-8; professional associations 9; professionals 61, 157, 180
profits 83, 89, 93, 97, 186
proletariat 56
property 48, 89
protection 166, 169, 171-2, 174
public sector 14, 45-6, 50, 60-2, 110, 112-13, 123, 190
public sector borrowing 14, 17-18, 31, 181

quasi-professionals 117-20
queuing 43, 119

Rate Support Grant 160, 190
rationalism 36, 49, 68-9, 73, 75-6, 196
'real' economy 15, 18, 90
regions 78, 123, 138, 160-1, 184, 186, 189
relational economics 22-3, 203
rentier class 138, 143
repentence 77, 198
revelation 68-9
Ricardo, David 58
righteousness 72, 76, 183
Robbins, Lionel 11, 36
Ruskin, John 48
Russia 55, 78n, 154

Samuelson, Paul 39
savings 17, 41, 85-90, 141-4
Schumacher, Fritz 78n
Second World War 38, 53, 111-12, 170
seigniorage 89-90, 184
self-criticism 69, 195-8
self-interest 30, 45, 57, 69-70, 72, 97, 104-5, 117, 126-7, 150-1, 174, 180
self-justification 77, 196-8
service 55, 78-80, 98-106, 109, 111, 124-5, 127
shareholders 91-3, 111-13, 184-5
sin 19, 76-7
Smith, Adam 5, 57, 100
Social Democratic Party 9
Social Security 36, 150, 153
Socialism x, 1-2, 6, 13-15, 53-63, 67, 154, 179, 191
stability 21, 23
State: in general 14, 59-61, 63, 74-5, 123-6, 149-62, 193;